The World's Embrace

ABDELLATIF LAÂBI

The World's Embrace

SELECTED POEMS

Edited, with an Introduction by Victor Reinking
Foreword by Ammiel Alcalay
Translations by Anne George, Edris Makward,
Victor Reinking, and Pierre Joris

City Lights Books
San Francisco

Poems copyright © 1992, 1993, 1996 by La Différence
Foreword copyright © 2003 by Ammiel Alcalay
Introduction and editorial matter copyright © 2003 by Victor Reinking
Translations copyright © 2003 by Anne George, Edris Makward, Victor
Reinking, and Pierre Joris

These poems were first published in *Le Soleil se meurt* (1992), *L'Etreinte
du monde* (1993), and *Le Spleen de Casablanca* (1996) by La Différence
Editions Littéraires et Artistiques, Paris, with the exception of "La terre
s'ouvre et t'accueille" (copyright © 2003 by Abdellatif Laâbi).

10 9 8 7 6 5 4 3 2 1

Cover design: Robin Raschke and Amy Trachtenberg
Book design and typography: Harvest Graphics
Editor: Robert Sharrard

This work, published as part of the program of aid for publication,
received support from the French Ministry of Foreign Affairs and the
Cultural Service of the French Embassy in the United States. Cet ouvrage
publié dans le cadre du programme d'aide à la publication bénéficie du
soutien du Ministère des Affaires Etrangères et du Service Culturel de
l'Ambassade de France aux Etats-Unis.

Library of Congress Cataloging-in-Publication Data

Laâbi, Abdellatif, 1942-
    [Poems . English. Selections]
    The world's embrace ; selected poems / by Abdellatif Laâbi ;
translated by Victor Reinking, Anne George and Edris Makward
        p.   com
    ISBN 0-87286-413-8 (pbk.)
    I. Reinking, Victor W.   II. George, Anne O.   III. Makward, Edris.
IV. Title.
PQ3989.2.I.23 A6 2003
841'.914—dc21   2002073845

CITY LIGHTS BOOKS are edited by Lawrence Ferlinghetti and Nancy J.
Peters and published at the City Lights Bookstore, 261 Columbus Avenue,
San Francisco, CA 94133. Visit our Web site at www.citylights.com

Contents

The initials of the translators are set in brackets.
They are as follows:

A. G.   Anne George
E. M.   Edris Makward
V. R.   Victor Reinking
P. J.   Pierre Joris

FOREWORD

WRITING THE BODY COLLECTIVE:
ABDELLATIF LAÂBI'S VISIONARY POETICS

From our present perspective, as the media bombards us with an insidiously violent form of ignorance and misinformation and the United States government continues to reapportion the boundaries of the Middle East, it is almost inconceivable to think about the cultural space occupied from the late 1950s to the mid-1960s by texts sympathetic to and emerging from the cauldron of decolonization. Books like Henri Alleg's *The Question*, Pierre Bourdieu's *The Algerians*, Pierre Vidal Naquet's *Torture: Cancer of Democracy*, Simone de Beauvoir and Gisele Halimi's *Djamila Boupacha*, Albert Memmi's *The Colonizer and the Colonized*, Kateb Yacine's *Nedjma*, the writings of Frantz Fanon, Gillo Pontecorvo's film *The Battle of Algiers* — these and many other works were readily available and formed a critical mass of resources related to a contentious political reality that could neither be ignored nor theorized out of existence.

Some of our last stabs at radical internationalism may have been the efforts of the Black Panther Party, following in the footsteps of Malcolm X after his pilgrimage to Mecca, to establish diplomatic and cultural ties with newly independent states in Africa. It is tremendously ironic that, while the FBI's COINTELPRO program worked tirelessly to place an irreconcilable wedge between Jews and black Americans in the United States, the Moroccan Jewish theorist and future political prisoner Abraham Serfaty delivered a "salute to the African-Americans" at the 1969 Pan-African Cultural Festival in Algeria, a festival that Archie Shepp played at along with Tuareg musicians, long before the marketing strategies of World Music. But by this point, American soldiers were fighting amongst themselves almost as fiercely as they fought the enemy in Vietnam. Alliances splintered as the country divided itself bitterly over the ever more pointless last years of the war. Many veterans would return home to the charred ruins of deindustrialized cities and towns, drifting into drugs, drink, and homelessness. United States policy shifted completely toward Israel following the June war of 1967 — from that point on, almost everything coming in to the United States from the Middle East would be viewed through the filter of the Zionist narrative. Identity politics and nationalisms of all stripes came to dominate North

American discourse, eventually settling into a version of autistic multi-culturalism effectively cut off from access to useful forms of democratic power at the national level. The covert wars of the 1980s gave way to the first made for television, fought at prime time bonanza, the Gulf War. From 1990 until 9/11 and the assault on Afghanistan, Islam was reshaped to fit the mold of a ubiquitous and unyielding enemy. The new crusades were upon us.

Any attempt to retrieve the cultural and political complexities of the Arab world during this period is a formidable task, particularly because the United States, unlike France or England, has not carried out a direct and long-term colonial occupation in the region. And we remain incalculably impoverished because of the lingering and deep-seated effects of the Cold War's highly succesful recategorization of knowledge arranged according to the priorities of the military-industrial complex and the needs of American exceptionalism. At the same time, mainstream intellectuals are either frightfully ignorant about the Arab world or in service to the state, while too many seemingly more sophisticated academic thinkers hide behind a theoretical facade that remains but a shadow play of politics instead of an entrance onto other stages where politics might matter more.

How, then, in such a context, is one to introduce a figure as formidable as Abdellatif Laâbi? Poet, novelist, playwright, journalist, translator, editor, former political prisoner, both witness and visionary, Laâbi is a practitioner upon whose very body and spirit the aspirations of theory have been played out. As he writes of a human collective that has faced the depths of degradation: "We will need a nakedness / that even our skin cannot distort." It is this phenomenological sense of the radical nature of experience that Laâbi brings to his writing, a sense of the "infinite crumbling world." In the second issue of *Souffles*, the remarkable revolutionary journal that Laâbi edited from 1966 until it was closed down by Moroccan authorities in 1972 and Laâbi, along with many associated with the journal, were thrown into prison, he writes: "The act of writing cannot be dependent on formulaic recipes, nor can it concede to fashion, the teary-gas needs of rich demagogues or a quest for power. Poetry is all humans are left with to proclaim their dignity, to not fade into a mass, for their inspiration will remain imprinted forever to attest to the shriek."

In our world of specialized and professionalized activities, we have very few places to seek a context for Laâbi's utter confrontation with the historical world, with the wounds of memory the body has absorbed. In describing the unspeakable experiences of imprisonment and torture,

Laâbi truly reaches the zero degree of writing: "The sought after objective is the sterilization of the prisoner's senses, the disconnection from all relations (from other men, from nature, women, their own bodies) which had, beforehand, allowed them to situate themselves in reality, history, and play an active role. Prison writing is both a defense and an illustration of the human being, in a generic way. Because of this the [imprisoned] writer gives the impression of writing not for a determined audience but for humanity as a whole." By asserting the autonomy of the human spirit even under such conditions, Laâbi came to realize that "Prison for me was precisely this school for liberty." As we move further and further into the realms of "maximum security," we are, collectively, more than ever in need of this sense of liberty, this sense of poetry and poetry's possibilities to proclaim our dignity.

Ammiel Alcalay

INTRODUCTION

Abdellatif Laâbi has lived many lives and, from the time poetry first came to him, he has never stopped writing. Although his identity as a writer is deeply rooted in his poetic consciousness, the body of his work forms an extraordinary mosaic of genres and moods and commitments. In addition to twelve books of poetry, he has also published plays, novels, books for children, scores of political essays, two volumes of interviews, and a book of letters from prison. Throughout his working life—which now spans some forty years—he has also been active as a translator, and his superb French versions of major contemporary Arab authors (at last count, sixteen books) include, among many others, works by Palestinian poet Mahmoud Darwish, Moroccan poet Abdallah Zrika, Iraqi poet Abdelwahed Al Bayati, Syrian novelist Hanna Mina, and an anthology of thirty-six contemporary Palestinian poets.

In his native Morocco, where he was born in 1942, Laâbi's stature has become that of national poet, yet it is only recently that he has been officially rehabilitated there, after spending most of the 1970s in prison—for his poetry, and for the militant stances of *Souffles*, a literary journal he founded and directed. He left for Paris in 1985, and spent the rest of the 1980s and 1990s there, as an exile. But "prison poet" or "exiled poet" are labels Laâbi has steadfastly refused; his itinerary remains one of constant movement, and becoming.

By his own account, Laâbi had a happy childhood. He spent his formative years in the medina (old city) of Fez, his father a skilled artisan—a saddle maker—his mother a wise, loving presence in his life. Yet early on he found himself caught between two historical demons: the French colonial regime of his youth, with its institutionalized cultural schizophrenia and racism, and the increasingly tyrannical reign of King Hassan II, whose initial tolerance for free-thinking intellectuals and radical poets soon evaporated.

In his early writing, like many gifted young poets living through seismic social upheavals, the passion of his political stance made for poetry that was deeply colored by polemics, and outrage at the local corruption, injustices, and petrified thinking that had superceded colonial oppression. The poems in his first collections, *Le Règne de Barbarie* (The Reign of Barbarism) and *Poèmes oraux* (Oral Poems), both published in the 1960s, vibrate with anger and revolt, and sometimes sound like a poetic elaboration of Frantz Fanon's notion of purification through violence. In a 1972 interview with the magazine *Jeune Afrique* (published after his initial arrest, interrogation, and torture, but prior to his definitive imprisonment), Laâbi summed up the driving force, and dilemma, that propelled him and other young Maghrebin writers of the time:

> Our generation was the generation of independence, of the will for decolonization, of the cry similar to that of a Frantz Fanon in his book *The Wretched of the Earth*. A generation that rediscovered the enormous creative energy of the people, within the enthusiasm of the beginnings of liberation. Then, quickly, a generation of disillusion, of nightmares, of false independences, of semantic drama, of the spectacle of resignation and deterioration, but also of the radicalization of hopes.

Poems such as "Etat de violence" (State of Violence), "Marasmes" (Stagnations), "Gloire à ceux qui nous torturent" (Glory to Those Who Torture Us), "Vie urgente" (Urgent Life), and "Les singes électroniques" (Electronic Monkeys) career across the page with a furious exuberance and a collision of meanings; it is, by turns, a poetry that screams, that unloads anarchic images and pulses with a frenzied originality, and that embraces the indispensable role of the poet as awakener. At the end of the long poem "Demain le séisme" (Tomorrow the Upheaval), for example, Laâbi delivers his poetic credo of that time:

les ennemis de mon peuple
on failli tuer la poésie en moi
j'ai tellement crié crié crié
j'ai tellement saigné saigné saigné
cri et sang était devenue ma poésie
mais maintenant
je la veux étincelle
qui puisse mettre le feu
à toute la plaine
je la veux muscle, arme
je la veux rues et places
je la veux millions de gosiers
deversant la haine
de l'oppression

the enemies of my people
almost murdered the poetry in me

so much did I scream scream scream
so much did I bleed bleed bleed
scream and blood had become my poetry
but now
I want it to be a spark
that might ignite
the whole plain
I want it muscular, a weapon
I want it to be streets and squares
I want it to be millions of throats
pouring out hatred
of oppression

In 1965, Laâbi led a group of young writers in founding the journal *Souffles*, the collected issues of which (1966–72) represent a major cultural monument in Moroccan, and indeed African history. The goals of the *Souffles* project were ambitious: Laâbi and his colleagues (principally Moroccan poets Mohammed Khaïr-Eddine and Mostapha Nissaboury, in the beginning) set out to reinvent the cultural and ideological landscape of postcolonial Maghreb. Along the way, they not only challenged the forms of artistic and political expression inherited from Europe but also the stagnation and constrictions brought on by what Laâbi called an "interior colonialism." The *Souffles* generation of the 1960s and '70s, as he stated at the time, ". . . never hesitated to desecrate the untouchable sanctuaries such as language, and a certain cultural ethics, and to challenge, with an equal violence, the pretensions of a certain West to dictate to other peoples its values and formulas, as well as the false values and fossilized outlooks of our own culture."

The *Souffles* project, along with a parallel, Arabic-language journal, *Anfas*, came to a violent end in 1972 when Laâbi and other Moroccan intellectuals were arrested, tortured, and imprisoned. The poetry and prose written during his imprisonment and the two or three years following his release constitute an important second phase of Laâbi's work. From the crucible of incarceration and the shock of return flowed poetry, letters, and a novel. The works from this period (1973–82) include *L'Arbre de fer fleurit* (The Iron Tree Is Flowering), *Chroniques de la citadelle d'exil* (Chronicles from the Citadel of Exile), *Historie des sept crucifiés de l'espoir* (Story of Seven Crucifixions of Hope), *Sous le bâillon, le poème* (Beneath the Gag, the Poem), and his celebrated, prose/poetry account of prison and return, *Le Chemin des ordalies* (The

Path of Ordeals, published in English translation as *Rue du Retour*), about which South African poet Breyten Breytenbach wrote (in the preface to the English version) "...the book itself is a flame—because it is both the description of an ordeal and its burning away until the essentials are laid bare, a torture and a purification, illuminating a life and transforming it to the lightness of being, so that the book becomes both the illustration and the incarnation of its own existence."

There is a brutal immediacy to much of the writing from this period, but Laâbi found a way to raise the literary stakes of his work, and succeeded in distilling a kind of essence of incarceration, a poetics of prison. In 1985 he wrote:

As for the approach I took to my experience of prison, I could have drifted into an almost canonized genre: the series of portraits, the humiliations, the physical and psychological suffering, etc. But what concerned me most—beyond these realities, which I have not evaded—was to account for the way in which a man could "function" in such conditions: the extraordinary expansion of his inner world, his haunting encounter with himself, the atrophy of some of his faculties combined with the heightening of others, his waking and sleeping dreams, and, perhaps more than all of that, the way in which a man, cast into a situation he had not foreseen or even imagined, gradually manages to infuse it with his own values, to humanize it, to lend it a certain rationality—in short, to break through the prison's bars, even the supposedly unbreakable system itself, by summoning up his human ingenuity, his capacities to adapt, to give of himself, to love . . .

And at the end of a poem included in the 1990 collection, *Tous les déchirements* (All the Tearings), dedicated to Nelson Mandela and Abraham Serfaty, he retraces one arc of the prison experience, probes its inner trajectory:

Un homme est en prison
Il n'attend pas
il n'a pas de temps à perdre
Il se fait peintre et poète et musicien
Il invite le papillon des mots
à la transe qui fait pousser des racines
Il réfute le sobriquet des couleurs
pour que le blanc de la toile
libère ses démons tapis

Il ravive le cri du silence
pour orchestrer la symphonie du don

A man is in prison
He is not waiting,
he has no time to lose,
He becomes a painter, a poet, a musician.
He invites the butterfly of words
to the trance that makes roots grow.
He refutes the alias of colors
to allow the white of the canvas
to liberate its embedded demons.
He revives the scream of silence
to orchestrate the symphony of giving

In much of the poetry from what might be called a third phase of his work, beginning, roughly, in 1985–86 with *Discours sur la colline arabe* ("Discourse on the Arab Hill") and *L'Ecorché vif* ("Skinned Alive") and continuing to the present, Laâbi has further expanded his poetic range and moods. The tones and subjects and diction of his later poetic projects vary widely, and he moves with ease from the elegiac to the whimsical, or from the intensely personal to the proverbial. Much of his longer works, including several included in this volume, are poems of witness and remembrance and, in prophetic moments, reflect a vision of the whole teeming, suffering human continent in its quest for healing and harmony. There is a different music to this poetry than in his earlier work, different silences and often a deeper darkness. But there is also light seeping through, in the spaces between what Laâbi describes as "the madness of hope and the backlash of despair." French poet Lionel Ray wrote of Laâbi's later work that "There is a directness to the writing, and the clarity of what cannot and should not be said differently: nothing excessive, nothing approximate, a precise and tender approach to what is essential . . . and always this faith in the most beautiful of poetry's functions—a celebration of the ephemeral."

Although he writes in French—the language imposed by the educational system upon his generation of writers—he remains a quintessentially Arab writer concerned, throughout his work, with the heritage, history, and aspirations of both his native Morocco, and of what some have called the Arab nation: the constellation of widely diverse lands linked by their shared language. His personal history has made him a true bilingual, and within his French texts, one often senses rhythms of a different cultural music. Laâbi elaborated on this point in a lecture he gave in Germany in 1991:

What is the function of the Arabic language in my work? First of all, there are two Arabics. In what I write, there is a classical, or literary Arabic and there is also the maternal Arabic, the dialectical Arabic of Morocco. These two levels of language have a definite place in what I write. Poetry is an exercise in which the subconscious plays a crucial role. Everything within the personality of the writer that is linked to his childhood, his memory, his cultural roots, resurfaces in a dramatic way in whatever he writes. I have the feeling that, whenever I write in French, the two Arabic languages speak inside my text. They speak through their smells, their colors, their particular rhythms, and through the very sonorousness of their words. All of the human experience which was mine in these two languages flows into my texts.

One recurring element in Laâbi's poetry, as in much of his prose and dramatic writing, is the dialectic between chaos and cosmos, in which the poet is both the "statistician of pain" and "the fool of hope." The chaos is the world's, and his own, yet as he charts his often violent confrontations — with history, with tyrants and torturers, with atrophied thinking, with himself — his itinerary persistently weaves back to hope and transcendence, love and laughter.

The poems in this book were selected by Laâbi from three collections written in the 1990s: *Le Soleil se meurt* (1992), *L'Etreinte du monde* (1993), and *Le Spleen de Casablanca* (1996). For reasons of space, some of the initial choices had to be eliminated, but what remains is a fair representation of an important part of Laâbi's work from this period. As for the translations, while we have not limited ourselves to a doomed attempt at word-for-word exactness, we have nonetheless avoided wholesale adaptations and have attempted to remain as close to the original as possible. It is our hope that these versions will be but the first attempts to bring more of the works of this remarkable poet into English.

Victor Reinking

The World's Embrace

SELECTED POEMS

ÉLOGE DE LA DÉFAITE

Ce matin plus calme
Les bourgeons s'enhardissent
pas les mots
encore blessés
souillés
Une mouche seule
fait le printemps

La mort s'est lassée

Même la paix est laide

Loin du corps qui fut
le sang rampe
entre les rives dévastées
du cœur

Babylone
a détruit
Babylone

The Sun Is Dying

IN PRAISE OF DEFEAT

This calmer morning
The buds grow bolder
not words
still wounded
defiled
A single fly
makes the spring

Death has grown weary

Even peace is ugly

Far from the body that was
blood slithers
between the ruined shores
of the heart

Babylon
has destroyed
Babylon

Que s'édifie
le Mur de l'Hilarité !
On viendra
s'y cogner le front
les dents
le sexe
On crèvera de rire
jusqu'au dernier
si cela peut soulager la terre

Ah je l'ai arpentée
cette terre
Partout imploré
le ciel humain
Et maintenant
parfois je trouve
que ma cellule
m'a été plus clémente

L'arbre
peut-il mentir
lui aussi?

D'une cohue l'autre
je cherche les yeux
qui cherchent les miens
Les passants
ont-ils encore des yeux?

La peur de vivre
a remplacé
la peur de mourir

May the wall of Mirth
be built!
We'll come
and bang our heads there
our teeth
our sexes
We'll die laughing
to the last one
if that will sooth the earth

Ah I've paced it up and down
this earth
Everywhere implored
the human sky
And now
at times it seems
my cell
was more lenient

Can
the tree
lie too?

From one crowd to the next
I seek the eyes
seeking mine
do passersby
still have eyes?

The fear of living
has replaced
the fear of dying

Assis sur la chaise de Van Gogh
devant un bûcher froid
je me tords l'oreille
et défie les tournesols

L'amour s'insinue
et dit :
Si je déserte
que restera-t-il ?

Les pluies
ne tarderont pas
Elles rouleront leur acide
sur l'ardoise des toits
noirciront les bagues
aux doigts des forsythias
La menace des nuages
se confirme

Derrière les nuages affairés
le miroir brûle
comme un torchon

Ah mon frère
mon semblable
Tu es donc ainsi ?

Les mots me fuient
Je partage leur méfiance

Seated on Van Gogh's chair
facing a cold fireplace
I twist my ear
and challenge the sunflowers

Love creeps in
and says:
If I walk out
what will remain?

The rains
will come soon
They'll roll their acid
on the roof slates
blacken the rings
of forsythias' fingers
The threat of clouds
is real

Behind the busy clouds
the mirror is burning
like a rag

Ah my brother
my fellow human
Is that how you are?

Words flee from me
I share their distrust

Mais que faire
quand ce sont les morts qui lancinent
Rien d'audible
Juste un signe
de sous les décombres
« Enterrez-nous dignement ! »

La guerre
dites-vous
Quelle guerre ?

Voilà
je démissionne du genre humain
Je vais me faire chien
ou plutôt chienne
Je vais apprendre à flairer
le mal
de loin
de très loin

Si les chiens me rejettent
je demanderai aux magnolias
de m'accepter pour fleur
le temps que dure
une fleur de magnolia

Sinon
j'irai me terrer dans une fourmilière
Réapprendre ce qu'est le travail
invisible
que les géants écrasent
plus ou moins par mégarde

But what can I do
when the dead insist
Nothing audible
Just a sign
from beneath the rubble
"Bury us with dignity!"

The war
you say
What war?

There
I resign from the human race
I'll become a dog
or rather a bitch
I'll learn to sniff out
evil
from far
very far away

If the dogs won't have me
I will ask the magnolias
to accept me as a flower
for the time a magnolia
flower endures

Otherwise
I'll go to ground in an anthill
Relearn the invisible work
that giants crush
more or less inadvertently

J'irai de l'autre côté
Celui où le temps n'est pas une machine
à broyer la vie
Celui où l'espace
n'est pas un obstacle à la vue
Là où je me confondrai
avec un corps aimant-aimé
qui n'a point enfanté
et qui n'a point été enfanté

Je serai l'ermite invisible
l'instrument du désert

Je serai bref
et entier
pour ne pas rompre l'harmonie
de l'univers

Ah j'aimerai
d'amour
le seul être
que je n'ai pas entendu blasphémer
le nom de l'homme

Elle m'aura rejoint
dans ma petitesse
mon aimée aux ongles rongés
et nous vivrons jusqu'à la fin
d'une goutte d'eau
et d'une amande

I will cross over
to the other side
Where time is not a machine
for crushing life
Where space
is not an obstacle to sight
Where I will merge
with a beloved-loving body
that has not given birth
that has not been born

I will be the invisible hermit
the desert's tool

I will be brief
and whole
so as not to break the harmony
of the universe

Ah I will love
truly
the only being
I have not heard blaspheme
the name of man

She will have joined me
in my smallness
my beloved with the chewed fingernails
and we will live until the end
on a drop of water
and an almond

Partagerez-vous
un rêve
si menu ?

Non
le temps n'est pas au rêve
C'est impudique un rêve
et inutile
comme les larmes du poète

Il n'y a de monde
que ce monde-ci
A lui nous appartenons
et à lui nous retournons
Que sa raison soit sanctifiée
Que son règne demeure

Il y a tout dans ce monde
tant décrié
Le soleil, la lune
les vaches, les cochons
la mer, la glèbe
l'amour, la haine
la joie, la tristesse
la paix, la guerre
les hauts et les bas
Que voulez-vous donc de plus ?

Ce monde n'est pas parfait
mais c'est le seul qui existe
Trouvez-nous-en un autre !

Will you share
such a tiny
dream?

No
this is not a time for dreams
A dream is indecent
and useless
as the poet's tears

The only world
is this world
To it we belong
and to it we return
Hallowed be its reason
May its reign endure

There's everything in this world
so demeaned
The sun, the moon
the cows, the pigs
the sea, the soil
love, hatred
joy, sadness
peace, war
ups and downs
What more do you want?

This world isn't perfect
but it's the only one there is
Find us another one!

Si j'avais des réponses
je ne me brûlerais pas aux questions

Je voudrais croire
à la réalité de mon corps
de ses besoins
Mais je ne sais d'où vient
cette voix
qui se refuse aux apparences

Je voudrais me soumettre
corps et âme
comme une femme
ou comme un homme
converti à l'amour

Je voudrais dormir
un siècle ou deux
et me réveiller
avec d'autres idées
d'autres passions
Mon troisième œil bien ouvert
au front
ou mieux dans la nuque

Je voudrais
chaque fois que j'ouvre la main
dans mon sommeil
qu'une main anonyme
s'insinue dans la mienne
et m'invite
par petites pressions universelles

If I had answers
I wouldn't burn with questions

I would like to believe
in the reality of my body
its needs
But I don't know where
this voice begins
that says no
to appearances

I would like to surrender
body and soul
like a woman
or a man
converted to love

I would like to sleep
a century or two
and wake up
with other ideas
other passions
My third eye wide open
in my forehead
or better still
the nape of my neck

I would like
each time I open my hand
in my sleep
an anonymous hand
to steal into mine
and invite me
with little nudges

au partage d'un repas
qui ne serait pas celui de la trahison

Je voudrais
sortir maintenant de ma chambre close
et trouver au tournant de la rue
Saïda Menebhi[1]
plus vivante que quand elle était vivante
tenant par la main une petite fille
qui lui ressemblerait comme deux gouttes d'eau
Et la petite fille
me tendrait une orchidée noire
en disant : Ça, c'est pour la peine du poète

Je voudrais
qu'un oiseau-rokh
vienne m'empoigner sans ménagement
me fasse voler dans les airs
et me dépose dans ce pays
où la vallée des roses
aurait absorbé la vallée des larmes
Maroc mien
que je dénommerais Levant de l'âme

Je voudrais abattre le conditionnel
et dire au présent :
Lève-toi Lazare
la vraie vie t'attend

---

[1]Militante, compagne de détention. Morte en 1977 lors d'une grève de la faim.

to share a meal
that wouldn't be
the meal of betrayal

I would like
to leave my closed room now
and find Saïda Menebhi[1]
at the street corner
more alive than when she was alive
holding the hand of a little girl
who would be her mirror image
And the little girl
would give me a black orchid
saying: This is for the poet's pain

I would like
a mythic bird
to snatch me up
fly me across the sky
and set me down in the country
where the valley of roses
has swallowed the valley of tears
my Morocco
that I would name Levant of the soul

I would like to beat down
the conditional and say
in the present tense:
Arise Lazarus
real life is waiting

---

[1]Author's note: Activist, fellow prisoner. Died in 1977 during a hunger strike.

Je voudrais
m'arrêter d'écrire
sans avoir mauvaise conscience

O nuages immaculés
Ne partez pas
Soyez cléments
En vain je vous livre ma planche
pour que vous effaciez le cauchemar
et me fassiez jouir
de l'oubli
En vain

Je suis
la proie
de moi-même

J'arrache
et je bouffe
Jette les os
derrière mon épaule gauche
Et ça n'en finit pas

A croire
qu'un géant masochiste et paresseux
a choisi de m'habiter
pour que je fasse à sa place
cette triste besogne

Mais nul corps
n'est incessant
L'infini

I would like
to stop writing
without feeling guilty

O immaculate clouds
Don't leave
Be gentle
In vain do I hand over
my writing tablet
to erase the nightmare
and give me the bliss
of forgetting
In vain

I am
the prey
of myself

I tear away
and wolf down
Toss the bones
over my left shoulder
And there's no end to it

As though
a masochistic, lazy giant
decided to inhabit me
so I'd do this sad work
for him

But no body
is unremitting
The infinite

c'est ce qui le relie
à la banale souffrance

La guerre
dites-vous
Quelle guerre ?

Celle-là
qui se déroule sous nos pieds
aphasiques
bien avant Caïn
Ah quand l'ennemi se découvrit
dans la matière cannibale
Le sec contre l'humide
Le dur contre le friable
Pousse-toi que je m'y mette
Arbres titans contre tritons de laves
Gaz contre gaz
Le vaste dessin animé
de la Création
Dieux jaloux
déesses perverses
lois d'adultère et d'inceste
Chaos enfantant le chaos
Prix de l'ordre

La guerre
dites-vous
Quelle guerre ?

Celle-là
qui va de la graine au pain
du nuage au verre de thé
du regard oblique
au poignard dans le dos

is what links it
to trivial suffering

The war
you say
What war?

That one
unfolding beneath our
aphasic feet
long before Cain
Ah when the enemy found
the cannibal within
Dry against wet
Hard against flaky
Move over so I can get on with it
Titanic trees against lava tritons
Gas against gas
The vast animated cartoon
of Creation
Jealous gods
perverse goddesses
laws of adultery and incest
Chaos engendering chaos
The price of order

The war
you say
What war?

That one
which goes from the seed to the bread
from the cloud to the cup of tea
from the sidelong glance
to the knife in the back

de la caresse
à la strangulation
du berceau à la tombe
L'homme empêtré
dans ce nœud de pulsions
Victime
bourreau
bourreau du bourreau
et qui ne sait où donner du cœur
de la tête
vaincu chaque fois
se donnant des airs de vainqueur

Et que dire de l'enfant
qui ne sait que regarder ?

Viens mon enfant
Baptise ton aïeul
convertis-le à ton regard muet
Verse dans sa paume
quelques gouttes du baume

La guerre
dites-vous
Quelle guerre ?

Appelons-la
« Guerre des Arabes »
On pourra ainsi
plus tard
y faire allusion

from the caress
to strangulation
from cradle to grave
Man entangled
in this knot of urges
Victim
executioner
executioner of the executioner
and who doesn't know where
to put his heart
or his head
defeated each time
strutting like a conqueror

And what to say of the child
who can only look on?

Come my child
Baptize your ancestor
convert him to your quiet gaze
Pour a few drops of balm
in his palm

The war
you say
What war?

Let's call it
"The War of the Arabs"
so we can
refer to it later

Est-ce le soleil qui se lève
ou l'ultime lueur
d'un astre qui s'éteint ?

Ils ont refermé le livre
du désert
revêtu les longs manteaux
de la ressemblance
décrété la chasse à l'homme
sur toute la planète

Ils se sont improvisés juges
avocats
jurés
Ils ont rempli la salle
de leurs sbires
et fait vider le box des accusés

Ils ont divisé
le père et la mère
la sœur et le frère
l'amant et l'amante

Ils ont détourné
le fleuve
de la vérité

Et toi
perdu
au milieu de cette clameur toxique
titubant dans la fournaise
Homme lointain

Is that the sun rising
or the last fading light
of a dying star?

They have closed the book
of the desert
they have donned long cloaks
of resemblance
decreed a manhunt
all over the planet

They have appointed themselves judges
lawyers
jurors
They have filled the courtroom
with their henchmen
and emptied the defendants' dock

They have divided
father from mother
brother from sister
lover from lover

They have diverted
the river
of truth

And you
lost
in the midst of this toxic uproar
staggering in the furnace
Distant being

n'ayant plus de l'homme
ni la qualité
ni la quantité
Hirsute
dans la bourrasque délétère
Maintenant que le ciel a disparu
que reste-t-il à tes yeux
ton index
pour invoquer la miséricorde ?
Qui te croira
même si tu blasphèmes
et dis : J'ai vu l'enfer
Dieu en est innocent ?
On te clouera à tes atavismes
ta fatalité
et tu n'en seras pas
à ta dernière leçon
Il te faudra de nouveau
te couvrir de l'antique manteau
sous la neige et la lave
les huées et les insultes
répéter à voix basse
jusqu'à l'évanouissement
ton credo suspect
Pleure mon ami
tu n'en seras pas plus méprisé
Et cela fait du bien

O vaincus de tous les temps
voici venir l'ère
de votre humble message
Prenez garde
Ne vous mettez pas en tête
d'écrire l'Histoire
Laissez-la aux vainqueurs
Racontez plutôt
ce que nous avons perdu
dans le dédale de l'aveuglement
Faites-le en énigmes

possessing now
neither the quality
nor the quantity
of humanity
Unkempt
in the pernicious squall
Now that the sky has disappeared
what remains for your eyes
your forefinger
to cry for mercy?
Who will believe you
even if you blaspheme
and say: I have seen hell
and is God innocent?
You'll be nailed to your atavisms
your fate
and that won't be
your last lesson
You will need
to cover yourself again
with the ancient cloak
under the snow and lava
in the din of hoots and insults
and repeat in a hushed voice
your suspicious creed
until you black out
Weep my friend
you won't be despised more for that
And it helps

O vanquished of all times
the era
of your humble message
is at hand
Beware
Do not take it upon yourselves
to write History
Leave that to the conquerors
Tell instead
what we have lost
in the labyrinths of blindness

contes, devinettes, charades
petits poèmes rimés ou en prose
N'écrivez rien
racontez
Que la parole s'emboîte dans le souffle
et remplisse la bouche
Qu'elle se déverse de vos lèvres
tantôt miel
tantôt coloquinte
Rendez sa vigueur
à la mémoire en miettes
sauvegardez-la
Et puis procréez
faites passer le message
Parlez au-dessus de la haine
de la rancœur
Couvrez-les de vos voix prophétiques
et des cendres de cette planète
qui se refroidit
et s'éteint
faute d'amour

Montlouis-sur–Loire, 1991

Do it with enigmas
tales, riddles, puzzles
little rhymed poems or in prose
Write nothing
tell
Let speech merge with your breathing
and fill your mouth
Let it flow from your lips
now honey
now colocynth
Restore the force
to the shattered memory
safeguard it
And then procreate
spread the message
Speak above hatred
above rancor
Cover them with your prophetic voices
and with the ashes of this planet
which is growing cold
and dark
for lack of love

Montlouis-sur–Loire, 1991

LE SOLEIL SE MEURT

Le soleil se meurt
une rumeur d'homme à la bouche
C'est une étrange soif
quand grisonnent les idées
et que l'amour
à peine commence

Qui parle
de refaire le monde ?
On voudrait simplement
le supporter
avec une brindille
de dignité
au coin des lèvres

O dieu
si tu es homme
frère de l'homme
renonce à tes mystères
sors de ta grotte
Dis à tes partisans
la vanité de leurs temples
Plonge-les dans la cécité
Lève l'étendard de la révolte
Joins-toi à ceux
qui n'ont que leurs chaînes
pour labourer le malheur
Viens donc
leur embrasser les pieds

THE SUN IS DYING

The sun is dying
a rumor of man
on its lips
It's a strange thirst
when ideas go grey
and love
is only just
beginning

Who's speaking
of remaking the world?
We would simply like
to endure it
with a twig
of dignity
at the corner of our mouths

O god
if you are man
brother of men
give up your mysteries
come out of your cave
Tell your partisans
the vanity of their temples
Plunge them into blindness
Raise the flag of revolt
Join those
who have only their chains
to plough the fields of
the calamity
Come then
and kiss their feet

Il faisait bon vivre
au fond du labyrinthe
La lumière s'inventait
au bout des doigts de l'aimée
Les larmes étaient des fruits
hors saison
Le beau une essence
qui flirtait avec la vérité
Immanquablement le flux
naissait du reflux
La promesse pérégrinait
à petits pas de gazelle
dans le désert obligé
Il y avait comme une blessure sacrée
où s'abreuvait la vision

Demain l'incertain
encore plus incertain que l'hier
Il faudra pour se rendre
au chevet du soleil
trouver les fleurs vivantes
les oranges non traitées
le sourire à peu près sincère
se présenter et dire
dans le charabia qui reste :
De quel mal souffres-tu ?
Est-il humain
rien qu'humain ?

Les barbares
nos semblables
Ils ont toujours craché sur les merveilles
pissé sur les livres
coupé les têtes savantes
répandu du sel
sur les ruines de Sodome
pour finir dans une alcôve

It was good living
in the gut of the labyrinth
Light invented itself
at the tips of the beloved's fingers
Tears were fruit
out of season
Beauty an essence
flirting with truth
Inevitably ebb
gave birth to flow
The promise migrated
with delicate steps of
a gazelle in the immutable desert
There was
a sacred wound
where vision slaked its thirst

Tomorrow's unknowing
deeper than yesterday's
To get to the sun's bedside
we'll have to find living flowers
organic oranges
a more or less sincere smile
introduce ourselves and say
in the gibberish that remains:
What are you suffering from?
Is it human
simply human?

The barbarians
our ilk
They always spat on wonders
pissed on books
hacked off learned heads
spread salt
on the ruins of Sodom
and ended up in a den
of pleasure

au milieu d'almées au pubis rasé
de devineresses naines
et d'eunuques hilares

L'époque est banale
moins étonnante que le tarif d'une prostituée
Les satrapes s'amusent beaucoup
au jeu de la vérité
Les déshérités se convertissent en masse
à la religion du Loto
Les amants se séparent
pour un kilo de bananes
Le café n'est ni plus ni moins amer
L'eau reste sur l'estomac
La sécheresse frappe les plus affamés
Les séismes se plaisent à compliquer
la tâche des sauveteurs
La musique se refroidit
Le sexe guide le monde
Seuls les chiens continuent à rêver
tout au long des après-midi et des nuits

Il y aura une grande attente
avant la dite résurrection
Et le fils de l'homme
rendu à l'illusion
s'écriera : Qu'ai-je ?
Et les anges
peseurs du bien et du mal
s'écrieront : Qu'a-t-il ?
Et le ciel restera muet
comme au temps de la grande attente

Il y aura ce grand feu de veille
qui éloigne les fauves
et rassemble ceux

amidst almahs with shaved pubes
and dwarf soothsayers
and eunuchs with frozen smiles

The times are trivial
less surprising than
what a whore costs
The satraps have good fun
with the game of truth
The disinherited have mass conversions
to the religion of Lotto
Lovers separate
for a pound of bananas
Coffee is neither more nor less bitter
Even water is indigestible
Drought strikes the most famished
Earthquakes delight in complicating
the work of rescuers
Music is getting cold
Sex leads the world
Only dogs still dream
all through the afternoons and nights

There will be a long wait
before the heralded resurrection
And the son of man
resigned to the illusion
will cry out: What's wrong with me?
And the angels
with their scales of good and evil
will cry out: What's wrong with him?
And the sky will remain silent
as in the time of the long wait

There will be a great bonfire
that keeps the beasts at bay
and gathers together those

qui vont découvrir l'outil
Et le griot aux paroles qui blessent
se lèvera et frappera sept coups
au gong en bois de la mémoire
Et l'homme qui va faire fondre le métal
bondira et crachera au visage du griot
Et la femme aux sept maris reconnus
jettera au feu l'enfant disputé

Il y aura
au fond d'une grotte ou d'un désert
le survivant attitré des holocaustes
catastrophes nucléaires
épidémies informatiques
D'aucuns imaginent déjà son bonheur
l'affublent de l'ingéniosité de Crusoé
l'incitent à quitter son trou
pour rééditer la genèse
faire sortir de sa cuisse la femelle
et concevoir
Mais lui finit par se coucher
se recouvrir de sable
Il décide d'entamer
la grève de la vie

Où est la faute
Dans les ongles sales du labeur
qui coupe l'homme
en deux parties inégales
Dans les yeux têtus de la fourmi
qui se bat avec le fardeau du monde
Dans la paume de l'enfant
fasciné par le chant de la braise
Dans la convalescence du soldat aveugle
revenu de l'enfer
Dans une vulgaire pomme croquée
au su de tous
Dans une vie scandaleusement courte
au vu de l'éternité

who will discover the tool
And the griot whose words wound
will rise up and strike seven times
the wooden gong of memory
And the man who is to melt the metal
will leap up and spit in the griot's face
And the woman with seven acknowledged husbands
will throw the contested child into the fire

There will be
deep in a cave or a desert
the accredited survivor of the holocausts
nuclear catastrophes
computer epidemics
Some already imagine his happiness
call him a clever Crusoe
encourage him to leave his hovel
to repeat genesis
take the female from his thigh
and conceive
But he ends up going to bed
covering himself with sand
He decides to go
on a life strike

Where is the blame
In the dirty fingernails of toil
that divide humans
into two unequal parts
In the stubborn eyes of an ant
battling with the world's burden
In the palm of a child
mesmerized by the ember's song
In the convalescence of a blind soldier
back from hell
In an ordinary apple crunched
in view of all
In a life appallingly brief
in light of eternity

Dans la révolte ou la dérision
Où est la faute ?

Personne ne parlera
dans la langue archaïque de l'âme
avec cette musique de cœur qu'on écorche
et ce murmure de larmes fendant la pierre
Avec ces mots taillés dans les racines
et le bec recourbé de l'aigle
Avec le tonnerre qui ricane
le feu qu'on avale et recrache
Avec la panique
et la promesse des sept fléaux
Avec l'étoile qui apparaît
et le délire qui fait sens
Avec la horde en prière
et les tyrans qui meurent
d'un étrange mal de tête
Mais où sont les prophètes d'antan ?

Ce siècle qui n'en finit pas
et le suivant qui devra compter
cent unités
pas une de moins
sans que l'on sache
s'il y a vraie vie
paradis quelque part
sans qu'un signe indique
s'il y a commencement ou fin
Mais où sont les apocalypses d'antan ?

Mais il faudra
une immense écoute
des yeux, de la langue
de la matrice
des sexes incandescents
Que les enfants se réveillent

In revolt or derision
Where is the blame?

No one will speak
in the archaic tongue of the soul
with the flayed music of the heart
and the murmur of tears cleaving the stone
With words engraved in roots
and the curved beak of the eagle
With the cackling thunder
the fire you swallow and spit out
With the panic
and promise of the seven scourges
With the star that appears
and the lunacy that makes sense
With the praying horde
and tyrants dying
from a strange headache
But where are the prophets of old?

This endless century
and the next which will
have one hundred units
not one less
without us knowing
if there is real life
paradise somewhere
with no sign to mark
a beginning or an end
But where are the apocalypses of old?

But we will need
a vast listening
of eyes, tongues
of the womb
incandescent sexes
Let children awaken

de leur naïve hibernation
Que les femmes reviennent
de leur double exil
Que les mâles se mettent enfin
en quête de leur identité
Il faudra qu'une soif inconnue
nous tenaille
Il nous faudra une nudité
que même la peau ne pourrait travestir

L'enfant s'éloigne
tirant avec une ficelle
son petit coffre en bois
Cercueil ou berceau ?
Il ne sait
Il marche
parce qu'on lui a parlé de la mer
comme d'un âge adulte de l'eau
et des îles
comme de villes de cristal
érigées dans un jardin
L'enfant s'éloigne
et sa tête blanchit
à la vitesse de la rumeur

Maître de la lumière
voici le désert
sa page impitoyable
et loyale
Etends tes doigts sur la flamme
et supporte
Puis écris la vague qui te tourmente
vocalise-la
Fais que ta main soit l'artisane
de cette migration amoureuse
dans le silence des braves
Ne te retourne pas
pour contempler ton œuvre

from their naive hibernation
Let women return
from their double exile
Let males finally begin
the quest of their identity
We will need an unknown thirst
to torment us
We will need a nakedness
that even our skin cannot distort

The child moves away
towing by a string
his small wooden box
Coffin or cradle?
He doesn't know
He is walking
because they told him the sea
was like grown-up water
and islands
like crystal cities
erected in a garden
The child moves away
and his head whitens
at the speed of rumor

Master of light
behold the desert
its ruthless and
faithful page
Hold your fingers over the flame
and endure
Then write the wave
that torments you
give it voice
Make your hand the artisan
of this loving migration
in the silence of brave ones
Don't turn around
to contemplate your work

Déjà le vent apocryphe
s'acharne sur la trace
et le désert lave sa planche
l'enduit de glaise
pour l'égaré
ton imprudent sosie
qu'une autre vague tourmente

La fenêtre est là
A quoi sert de l'ouvrir
tant qu'elle donnera sur une porte close
avec cet incroyable numéro
18611 ?
Il faut apprendre à vivre en enfer
avec les hétaïres sacrées
les imprécateurs bègues
les saints affectés de coïtus interruptus
les fourmis carnivores
que même Satan n'a pu suborner
Apprendre à jouer des coudes
pour étaler son tapis de prière
là où il y a urgence
de compassion

La fenêtre cédera un jour
lorsque les hommes n'y pourront rien
et qu'ils n'auront en guise de mains
que des moignons pourris
peu habiles à compter l'argent
Lorsqu'ils perdront la vue
à force d'éviter le regard de leurs semblables
Lorsque la bête les aura rongés
jusqu'à la corde de leur graisse d'orgueil
Lorsque la puanteur de leurs idées
fera fuir même les dieux
qu'ils ont calomniés d'existence

Already the apocryphal wind
furiously attacks the traces
and the desert cleans
its slate
coats it with clay
for the lost one
your careless double
tormented by another wave

The window is there
What's the use opening it
as long as it looks out
on a closed door
with this incredible number
18611?
You must learn to live in hell
with the sacred hetaera
the stammering cursers
the saints afflicted with coitus interruptus
the carnivorous ants
that even Satan couldn't bribe
Learn to elbow
your prayer rug into the spot
where there is an urgency
for compassion

The window will yield one day
when men can no longer impede it
and their hands are nothing
but rotted stumps
no good for counting money
When they lose their sight
from avoiding the gaze
of their fellow men
When the beast has gnawed
away at them, right down
to the fat of their pride
When the stink of their ideas
drives away even the gods
they have accused of existing

Sûr
que cette planète a la nausée
Elle n'en peut plus
de devoir dispenser
le message de rosée
les éblouissements
la rage des beautés
qu'on ne peut enfermer dans un nom
le bruissement de tout fragile
les fragrances d'oasis boréales
Mille riens invisibles
qui font lianes
autour du sexe écartelé
où éclot le nouveau-né
Sûr qu'elle n'a plus envie
d'être lyrique

Paix
ne serait-ce qu'une minute
pour rendre au matin
ce qui appartient au matin
l'offrande et l'allégeance
le sein dardant ses rayons
la salive attendrissant la chair
sous la dent
le fabuleux sourire des amants
délicieusement inconscients
Et bénie soit la tourmente !

Ah il ne s'agit pas d'oublier
Quoi qu'en pensent les poètes
nous avons été heureux quelques fois
Le simple mot de liberté
nous a fait pleurer comme des Madeleines
Des hommes comme nous
nous ont semblé être
des dieux de bonté et de miséricorde
Nous avons baptisé places et rues

Certain
that this planet is nauseated
She can't go on
having to lavish
the message of dew
the bedazzlements
the rage of beauty
that cannot be reduced
to a name
the rustling of everything fragile
the fragrances of boreal oases
A thousand invisible nothings
that grow into lianas
around the torn sex
where the newborn blossoms
Certain that she no longer wants
to be lyrical

Peace
if only for a minute
to return to the morning
what belongs to the morning
the offering and allegiance
the breast beaming its rays of light
saliva softening nibbled flesh
the fabled smile of lovers
exquisitely unconscious
And blessed be the turmoil!

Ah it's not about forgetting
Whatever poets may think
we've been happy at times
The simple word freedom
has made us weep
Men like us
seemed to us
gods of kindness and mercy
We have christened squares and streets

en autant de soleils fraternels
Nous avons laissé pousser barbe et cheveux
pour que la douceur soit autant virile
que féminine
Nous avons dansé, chanté, bu
et fait l'amour toute la nuit
sur la paillasse crasseuse
du vieux monde

Nous en avons aboli des murailles
des prisons
autour de nous
en nous
Nous en avons investi des citadelles
déplacé des montagnes
Et nous n'avons pas hésité
à balayer devant notre porte
au point d'être impitoyables
envers nous-mêmes
Nous avons refermé les livres
petits et grands
pour n'apprendre que de l'intuition
de nos blessures
Nous avons ouvert les yeux
sur notre planète si fragile
monté la garde autour de ses poumons
Ah nous en avons appris des choses
de nos défaites

Avec cependant ce doute
qui donne à l'espoir
l'amertume tonique de son ivresse
Avec cependant cet espoir
qui donne au doute
le lyrisme de sa méthode
Avec des hauts et des bas
des couples qui foutaient le camp
des enfants qui crachaient dans la soupe

with so many fraternal suns
We let our beards and hair grow
so that softness could be as masculine
as feminine
We danced, sang, drank
and made love all night
on the putrid mattress
of the old world

We've knocked down many walls
many prisons
around us
inside us
We've besieged many citadels
moved mountains
And we didn't hesitate
to sweep our own doorstep
even to the point of being
ruthless with ourselves
We closed the books
large and small
to learn from the intuition
of our wounds
We opened our eyes
onto our fragile planet
We set up guard
around its lungs
Yes, we've learned many things
from our failures

With yet this doubt
that lends hope
the bracing bitterness of its rapture
With yet this hope
that lends doubt
the lyricism of its method
With highs and lows
couples who got the hell out
children who spat in the soup

Avec des amis qui disparaissaient
et reparaissaient en nœud papillon
Avec des exclusions et contre-exclusions
Avec la bouillie des dogmes
dont il restait toujours quelque chose
Avec la fureur rentrée réveillant les ulcères
Nous avons tenu autant que possible
dans ce radeau de fortune

Le soleil se meurt
une rumeur d'homme à la bouche
Le chaos viendra balayer la scène
de cette vieille tragédie
racontée mille et une fois
par un idiot
devant une salle vide
Ce sera une autre éternité
d'absence trouble
de duel entre masques
et de manque à écrire

Créteil, 1990

With friends who disappeared
and reappeared in bow ties
With exclusions and counter-exclusions
With the gruel of dogmas
of which there were always leftovers
With the suppressed rage that rekindles ulcers
We have held as steady as possible
in this makeshift raft

The sun is dying
a rumor of man
on its lips
Chaos will come and sweep the stage
of this old tragedy
told a thousand and one times
by an idiot
in an empty theater
It will be another eternity
of murky absence
of dueling masks
and lack of writing

Créteil, 1990

SEUL L'AMOUR

Est-ce la dernière image
ou la première ?
Le corps de l'autre
étendu dans sa lumière
Avec ses mains croisées
toujours belles
L'heure est à l'aurore
au coq de la séparation
« Ne fais pas semblant de dormir »
dit-elle
« raconte-moi ton voyage »
La vie est entre les mains de l'homme
répond l'autre
et il se lève

Cette nuit
le même rêve les a visités
Ils ne s'en souviennent plus
mais en ont la certitude
s'étant réveillés
la main
dans la main
J'ai rêvé . . . dit-elle
Je sais . . . dit l'autre

C'est un nomade
et une sédentaire
Lui confond les villes
et jusqu'aux continents
s'embrouille dans les langues
parfois dans les femmes
Elle, connaît la place des choses
sait nommer chaque joyau du collier
lit dans les fleuves et les étoiles

JUST LOVE

Is this the final image
or the first?
The body of the other
stretched out in its light
With her hands crossed
still lovely
The time is dawn
the cock-crow of separation
"Don't pretend to sleep"
she says
"tell me about your journey"
Life is in our hands
replies the other
and he gets up

Last night
they had the same dream
They don't remember
but are sure of it
waking up
hand
in hand
I dreamed . . . she says
I know . . . says the other

He is a nomad
she a sedentary one
He confuses one city with another
even continents
gets tangled in languages
sometimes in women
She knows the place of things
can name each gem of a necklace
reads rivers and stars

et de son index humecté
éclaire les routes
Elle conduit la caravane

Ils vieillissent côte à côte
comme des enfants
Leur rire ne s'est pas cassé
malgré les rigueurs de l'époque
Parce qu'ils ne cachent pas leurs rides
leur peau a gagné en douceur
Ils se mangent des yeux
et se caressent à distance
devant leurs enfants
qui les menacent
d'un bébé

Ils ont connu la guerre
les guerres étranges
où chacun retourne l'arme
contre soi-même
On se coupe le petit doigt
devant l'autre
On se taillade une veine
On prend le butin
dans ses objets personnels
lettres, colliers, coupe-papier
On s'emprisonne
dans son propre silence
Et quand les larmes coulent
d'un seul sourire
on signe l'armistice

C'est un couple mixte
comme tous les couples de la Création
Rien ne manque à leur palette
des couleurs de l'homme
A chaque couleur

and with her moistened finger
lights up the roads
She is leading the caravan

They grow old side by side
like children
Their laughter is unbroken
in spite of the harshness of the times
Because they do not hide their wrinkles
their skin has softened
They gaze hungrily at each other
exchange caresses at a distance
in front of their children
who threaten them
with a baby

They have known wars
strange wars
where each turns his weapon
on himself
They cut their little finger
in front of each other
They slash a wrist
They take the plunder
of personal objects
letters, necklaces, paper cutter
They imprison themselves
in their own silences
And when tears flow
with a single smile
they make the truce

They are a mixed couple
like all couples of Creation
Their palette is missing
no human color
To each color

ils ont donné une odeur
et ils mangent goulûment les odeurs
Quand ils marchent et s'éloignent
leurs pas se confondent
dans le mystère de l'Un

Lui
la prépare discrètement à sa mort
Il veut la précéder
pour lui envoyer des lettres
de là-bas
tant il aime lui écrire des lettres
Il imagine déjà
la première missive postée
de nulle part
« Je vais bien
Tu sais que je m'adapte en tout lieu
Mais cette immense paix
me tourmente
J'ai envie d'écrire
Seulement voilà
même ici
ces satanés mots sont rebelles »

Il l'attend
quand elle croit qu'il s'éloigne
Dans les rues
de la ville étrangère
il ne sait plus marcher tout seul
regarde les vitrines pour elle
Il feuillette un journal
et saute aux notices nécrologiques
qu'il lui reproche de lire
Il dort mal
et dans le lit absurde de l'abstinence
c'est elle
la femme imprévue

they have given a smell
and they greedily devour the smells
When they walk and move apart
their footfalls merge
in the mystery of One

He
is quietly preparing her
for his death
He wants to go first
and send her letters
from the other side
he so loves writing to her
He can already imagine
the first missive mailed
from nowhere
"I'm fine
You know I can adapt anywhere
But this immense peace
torments me
I feel like writing
Yet once again
even here
these damned words are rebellious"

He is waiting for her
when she thinks he has drifted away
In the streets
of the foreign city
he no longer knows
how to walk alone
looks in the store windows
for her
He flips through a newspaper
and goes straight for the obituaries
he scolds her for reading
He sleeps badly
and in the absurd bed of abstinence
she is
the unexpected woman

Je ne me sens d'aucun pays
dit-elle
Je n'ai de racines nulle part
Peut-être là-bas
quand je venais taper
sur les grilles de la séparation
je me sentais une patrie
au creux de tes mains
condamnées à l'absence
Et maintenant
je vivrai partout
où cette patrie
ne s'éteindra pas de tes mains

Elle ne sait pas
camoufler les morsures
trouver des explications aux bleus
Leurs amours
sont de moins en moins chastes
Ils ont écarté les tabous
d'un revers de désir pur
Ils éclairent leurs miroirs conjugués
et répandent l'encens de leurs cris
Ils ne se soucient pas de savoir
si leurs messes
appartiennent à une religion

Ils rêvent des Indes
du Mexique
et d'une taverne en Argentine
où les dieux du tango
les reconnaîtront sur-le-champ
leur feront fête
L'un d'eux
surgi d'une séquence d'*El Sur*[1]
viendra s'asseoir à leur table

---

[1]Film argentin de Fernando Solanas

I don't feel I'm
from any country
she says
I have no roots anywhere
Maybe back there
when I used to pound
on the bars of separation
I felt at home
in the hollow of your hands
condemned to absence
And now
I will live everywhere
where this homeland
will not fade from your hands

She cannot
hide the bites
explain away the bruises
Their lovemaking
is less and less chaste
They have brushed aside the taboos
of a hidden pure desire
They light up their twinned mirrors
and spread the incense of their cries
They don't care to know
if their rites
belong to a religion

They dream of India
of Mexico
and a tavern in Argentina
where the gods of tango
will spot them straightaway
and celebrate their presence
One of them
straight from a scene in *El Sur*[1]
will sit at their table

---

[1]Argentine film by Fernando Solanas

sortira de son long manteau de vaquero
un livre du poète marocain
et leur dira :
Eh compañeros
c'est leur monde qui est petit
Le nôtre est grand
El más grande !

Qui s'est converti à l'autre
et quelle est cette religion
où l'on ne prêche
ni ne convainc ?
C'est comme quand on frotte une allumette
et la tend à l'autre
pour qu'il la souffle
A qui viendrait l'idée
de commenter ce mariage fugace
du souffle et du feu
cette rencontre obligée
des doigts et de la bouche ?

Elle s'est endormie la compagne
Elle ne mordille plus ses cheveux fourchus
et ne pianote plus sur le mur
absorbée par sa lecture
Elle s'est endormie sur son livre
ne laissant à la convoitise
désirante du compagnon
que le lobe de son oreille

Il l'écrit
et elle l'écrit
Le manuscrit
est un jardin
avec une vasque centrale
et des arbustes à tête de lutin

and pull from his long vaquero's cape
a book by the Moroccan poet
and say:
Eh compañeros
it's their world that's small
Ours is large
El más grande!

Who converted to the other
and what kind of religion is this
where they don't preach
or persuade?
It's like when you strike
a match
and hold it out to the other
to blow it out
Who would ever think
to comment on this fleeting marriage
of breath and fire
this inevitable encounter
of fingers and mouth?

She's gone to sleep, the companion
She no longer nibbles her frazzled hair
or drums her fingers on the wall
absorbed by her reading
She's fallen asleep on her book
leaving nothing for the lust
of her companion
but the lobe of her ear

He is writing it
and she is writing it
The manuscript
is a garden
with a fountain
and elf-headed bushes

Dans cette miniature très fouillée
on découvre aussi l'Alhambra
la muraille ocre
de l'une des prisons du royaume
un enfant de Palestine
crucifié
et une pochette de disque
de Victor Jara

Dans le train à compartiments
ils ne savent s'ils doivent s'asseoir
côte à côte
ou l'un en face de l'autre
Ils essaient les deux avantages
en espérant que le contrôleur passe
le compartiment se vide
la nuit tombe
pour pouvoir fermer la porte
tirer le rideau
et développer conséquemment
leur intimité

Il éprouve le besoin
de lui découvrir les pieds
Ah ils ne sentent pas vraiment bon
comme tous les pieds
Mais il s'en fascine
à les masser
attendrir
Il s'obstine à en recompter les doigts
comme s'il l'appelait
à descendre à ses pieds
—qu'il trouve assez beaux
fallait-il le dire—
les découvrir à son tour
et peut-être
les embrasser

In this carefully excavated miniature
one can also find the Alhambra
the ochre wall
of one of the kingdom's prisons
a child from Palestine
crucified
and a record jacket
of Victor Jara

In the train compartment
they don't know if they should sit
side by side
or facing each other
They explore the delights of both
hoping the conductor will pass by
and the compartment empty out
and night fall
so they can close the door
draw the curtain
and thus expand
their intimacy

He feels the need
to uncover her feet
Ah, they don't smell too good
like all feet
But he is dazzled by them
massaging them
softening them
He keeps counting the toes
as though he were calling her
to move down to his feet
—which he finds rather attractive
it should be noted—
uncover them in turn
and perhaps
kiss them

Ils n'ont pas d'âge
leur histoire monte et descend
à la nuit des temps
Ils résument les livres
les légendes
Ils n'ont pas inventé la poudre
découvert l'Amérique
— heureusement ! —
Ils sont conscients
et inconscients
Ils ne revendiquent rien
pour eux-mêmes
Ils se contentent d'être
dans le message innocent
du partage

Cette pomme pour toi
cette pomme pour moi
Cette pomme
pour l'absent à nos yeux
présent dans nos cœurs
Pleurez ô arbres
pierres
poissons
oiseaux
Que s'émeuve le pays
Qu'il dénoue ses entraves
se laisse pousser des ailes
et se glisse parmi nous

Que vienne le temps
non imaginé
converti à l'offrande
et la brûlure
quittant la planche froide des temps
pour notre lit fiévreux
continent à lui seul
mère de la mer

They are ageless
their story rises and falls
in the night of time
They sum up books
legends
They didn't set the world on fire
discover America
— luckily! —
They are conscious
and unconscious
They claim nothing
for themselves
It's enough to exist
inside the innocent message
of giving

This apple for you
this apple for me
This apple
for the one
absent from our eyes
present in our hearts
Weep O trees
stones
fish
birds
May the country rise up
May it loosen its shackles
let its wings grow
and glide in among us

May the unimagined
time come
converted to the offering
and the burning
leaving the cold plank of time
for our feverish bed
a continent unto itself
mother of the sea

père de la terre
pâtre des transports et dérives
trône des amants

Et s'il ne reste qu'un miracle
ce sera peut-être celui-là
gagné à la sueur de l'âme
arraché comme une rose
perdue dans un champ de mines
déterré d'un ciel
que la rare bonté
a su cacher
parmi les cieux livrés
au pillage rituel
O miracle orphelin

Montlouis-sur-Loire, 1991

father of the earth
shepherd of raptures and driftings
throne of lovers

And if only a single
miracle remains
perhaps it will be that one
won by the soul's sweat
plucked like a rose
lost in a minefield
unearthed from a sky
that the rare goodness
could hide
among the skies abandoned
to the ritual pillage
O orphan miracle

Montlouis-sur-Loire, 1991

L'Étreinte du monde

LES ÉCROULEMENTS

Regarde mon amour
ce monde qui s'écroule
autour de nous
en nous
Serre bien ma tête contre ta poitrine
et dis-moi ce que tu vois
Pourquoi ce silence ?
Dis-moi simplement ce que tu vois
Les étoiles contaminées tombent-elles
de l'arbre de la connaissance
Le nuage toxique des idées
nous submergera-t-il bientôt ?

Dis-moi ce que tu vois
Brûle-t-on déjà les livres sur les places publiques
Rase-t-on la tête des femmes avant de les lapider
Y a-t-il des processions d'hommes à cagoule
brandissant croix et cimeterres
Pourquoi ce silence, mon aimée
Sommes-nous sur une île flottante
ou voguons-nous sur une torpille
Sommes-nous seuls
ou enchaînés à d'autres frères d'infortune
Quel jour sommes-nous
Quelle heure est-il ?

Serre bien ma tête contre ta poitrine
et si tu peux
ouvre ton ventre et accueille-moi

The World's Embrace

CRUMBLINGS

My love look at
this world crumbling
around us
within us
Hold my head tightly against your breast
and tell me what you see
Why are you silent?
Just tell me what you see
Are contaminated stars falling
from the tree of knowledge
Will the toxic cloud of ideas
engulf us, soon?

Tell me what you see
Are they burning books in public squares
Are they shaving women's heads before stoning them
Are there processions of hooded men
waving crosses and scimitars
Why are you silent, my beloved
Are we on a floating island
or drifting on a torpedo
Are we alone
or chained to other brothers of misfortune
What is the day
What is the hour?

Hold my head tightly against your breast
and if you can
open your womb and welcome me

au creuset de ta force
Fais-moi remonter le fleuve
jusqu'à la source des sources
Replonge-moi dans la vasque de vie
et verse sur ma fontanelle
sept poignées d'orge
en fredonnant la chanson de Fayrouz
celle que tu chantes mieux qu'elle

Pourquoi pleures-tu
As-tu peur pour le monde
ou pour notre amour
Ne peux-tu rien pour moi ?
Alors dis-moi simplement ce que tu vois
De quel mal meurt-on aujourd'hui
Quelle est cette arme invisible qui extirpe l'âme
et le goût à nul autre pareil de la vie
Quelle est cette caravane qui dévore ses chameaux
et vide ses outres d'eau dans le sable
Quel est ce magicien
qui fait de la guerre un acte d'amour ?

Pourquoi ce silence
Crois-tu toi aussi que les mots sont si souillés
qu'ils ne servent même plus à demander son chemin
Crois-tu qu'il n'y a plus rien à dire
et que mes pauvres versets
ne sont que dérision sur dérision
Veux-tu que je me taise
pour te laisser regarder ces écroulements
dans la dignité du silence ?

Serre bien ma tête contre ta poitrine
et berce-moi
Dans le cocon soyeux de tes mains
ma tête se fera toute petite
Le gros abcès des idées crèvera
et je redeviendrai l'enfant d'un autre siècle
effrayé par le tonnerre
et qui se donne du courage
en ânonnant un vieil alphabet
à la lueur d'une bougie
dans la maison interdite de Fès

in the crucible of your strength
Make me swim upstream
to the spring of springs
Immerse me again in the basin of life
and pour upon my fontanel
seven handfuls of barley
while humming the song of Fayrouz
the one you sing better than her

Why are you crying
Do you fear for the world
or for our love
Can you do nothing for me?
Then just tell me what you see
From what sickness are we dying today
What is this invisible weapon tearing out our souls
and the taste, like no other, for life
What is this caravan that devours its camels
and empties its waterskins upon the sand
Who is this magician
who turns war into an act of love?

Why are you silent
Do you too believe that words are so defiled
they can no longer be used even to ask one's way
Do you believe that there is nothing more to say
and that my poor verses
are just derision heaped upon derision
Do you want me to be quiet
so you can look at these crumblings
in the dignity of silence?

Hold my head tightly against your breast
and cradle me
In the silky cocoon of your hands
my head will become very small
The swollen abscess of ideas will burst
and I will become again the child of another century
frightened by thunder
who finds his courage
by droning an old alphabet
in the forbidden house of Fez
by candlelight

près d'un brasero où brûlent encens et fenugrec
et éclate dans l'alun le mauvais œil
Berce cet enfant qui n'a point été bercé
afin qu'il revive et fasse revivre entre tes bras
un monde englouti, saccagé, volé
dont il ne reste
qu'un âcre parfum d'innocence

Pourquoi ce silence mon aimée
Ai-je réveillé en toi ta douleur tue
ou le même besoin d'être bercée
Celui d'une petite fille née dans une autre guerre
partie au-delà des mers
pour rencontrer le soleil de ses livres d'images
en caresser les fruits d'or dans un verger
gardé par des légionnaires ?

Toi ignorant ce vain tourment des racines
plus près de l'homme que de sa rumeur
apprenant vite les langues méprisées
sachant semer là où saigne la glèbe
planter là où l'arrachement s'acharne
Tout cela, en faisant mine de passer
avec la loyauté des oiseaux migrateurs
et ce vague à l'âme qui les déchire en douceur
entre nid et périple

Pourquoi pleures-tu
Est-ce pour ce monde englouti
ou pour ce monde qui s'écroule
Pour l'enfant ou pour l'adulte
Pouvons-nous choisir entre deux adieux
nous résoudre à l'adieu
alors que le miracle est là
nos pouls qui battent paisiblement
jouent leur symphonie
poignet contre poignet
même si les armes parlent
à la place des poètes ?
Serre bien ma tête contre ta poitrine
et dis-moi ce que tu vois

close to a brazier where incense and fenugreek are burning
and the evil eye bursts in the alum
Cradle this child who has never been cradled
that he may live anew and in your arms revive
an engulfed, pillaged, ravaged world
where nothing remains
but a bitter smell of innocence

Why are you silent, my beloved
Have I awakened your mute pain
or the same need to be cradled
Of a little girl born during another war
gone away beyond the seas
to meet the sun of her picture books
to caress their
golden fruits in an orchard
watched over by legionnaires?

You who ignore this vain torment of roots
closer to man than his echo
quickly learning despised tongues
knowing to sow where the soil bleeds
to plant where the uprooting goes on relentlessly
All this while pretending to pass through
faithful as migrating birds
with the same melancholy
that tears at them gently
between nest and journey

Why are you crying
Is it for this engulfed world
or for this world which is collapsing
For the child or for the adult
Can we choose between two farewells
resign ourselves to the farewell
when the miracle is here
our pulses quietly beating
playing out their symphony
wrist against wrist
even if weapons speak
instead of poets?
Hold my head tightly against your breast
and tell me what you see

avec l'œil que nous avons patiemment cultivé
au plus noir des ténèbres
quand les jours de l'année se comptaient à l'envers
quand le printemps nous dévorait le sexe
quand l'automne était une hirondelle de cire sur notre oreiller
quand l'été nous marquait au fer rouge dans ses fourgons
et l'hiver nous accordait une miette de miséricorde
Quand quelques mots d'amour lancés à travers les grilles
nous nourrissaient pendant une interminable semaine
Quand je souriais à la conquête de ton sourire
et que tu versais la larme que je me refusais
Quand je faisais sortir de ma tête un pigeon
pour que tu l'arbores fièrement sur ton épaule
dans les files d'attente

Dis-moi ce que tu vois
avec cet œil de chair et d'acier
familier des ténèbres
vieux comme la conscience
contempteur de l'oubli
témoin irrécusable
Pourquoi ce silence mon aimée
Cet œil ne peut s'éteindre, n'est-ce pas ?
Alors dis-moi ce que tu vois
A-t-on commencé à détruire Grenade
Les barbares sont-ils à nos portes
Comment sont les barbares
Parlent-ils une langue inconnue
Viennent-ils vraiment d'une autre galaxie
d'une autre dimension du temps
En quoi nous ressemblent-ils
Quoi en eux est si terrifiant ?

Dis-moi ce que tu vois
Le fleuve des images monte-t-il toujours
Pour quand prévoit-on le déluge
Se bat-on déjà aux abords de l'arche
Que fait-on des chevaux blessés
des enfants qui ne peuvent pas marcher
Les femmes ont-elles pris les armes à leur tour
Y a-t-il au milieu de la horde un prophète perdu ?

with the eye we have patiently adapted
in the deepest of darknesses
when the days were counted in reverse
when spring was consuming our sex
when fall was a wax-swallow on our pillow
when summer was branding us with its fire rakes
and winter granted us a crumb of mercy
When a few words of love tossed through iron bars
nurtured us through an endless week
When I smiled to conquer your smile
and you shed the tear I was denying myself
While I conjured a pigeon from my head
so that you could proudly display it upon your shoulder
while standing in the waiting lines

Tell me what you see
with this eye of flesh and steel
accustomed to darkness
ancient as conscience
despiser of forgetfulness
irrefutable witness
Why this silence, my beloved
This eye cannot be extinguished, can it?
So tell me what you see
Have they begun to destroy Granada
Are the barbarians at our gates
What are the barbarians like
Do they speak an unknown tongue
Do they really come from another galaxy
from another dimension of time
How do they resemble us
What is it about them that is so terrifying?

Tell me what you see
Is the river of images still rising
When is the flood predicted
Are people already fighting close to the ark
What are they doing with the wounded horses
with children who cannot walk
Have women in their turn taken up arms
Is there a lost prophet in the midst of the horde?

Pourquoi ce silence mon aimée
Me condamnerais-tu à devoir imaginer
ce que je n'aurais jamais accepté d'imaginer
dussé-je me crever les yeux
Comment aurais-je pu croire que j'exercerais un jour
le métier réprouvé du corbeau
ou même le sombre office du cygne
Moi l'artisan fils de l'artisan
laboureur de l'antique beauté
tisserand de l'espérance
veilleur de l'âtre jusqu'aux cendres
berger sans gourdin du troupeau
que je dressais contre le chien-loup
Moi l'artisan fils de l'artisan
guettant l'arc-en-ciel
pour ne pas me tromper sur les couleurs
en me fiant à leurs noms
les recueillant une à une
dans la marmite en cuivre de ma génitrice
comme autant d'épices rares
destinées aux joies humaines
au partage d'un repas qui ne devient licite
que si les pauvres le bénissent et l'honorent ?

Comment aurais-je pu croire
que ce rêve qui m'a converti à l'homme
deviendrait un cauchemar
que les héros de ma jeunesse
scieraient l'arbre de mon chant
que les livres où j'avais rencontré mes sosies
jauniraient au fond de ma bibliothèque
que mon errance vouée à la rencontre
manquerait à ce point du gobelet d'eau
et de la galette déposés au bord de la route
par Celui ou Celle qui veille sur l'errance ?

Comment aurais-je pu croire
au mirage d'un si beau chemin
aux chaînes d'un si fol horizon
au ver dans un si beau fruit
Où donc était la faille ?

Why are you silent, my beloved
Would you condemn me to imagine
what I would never have conceded to imagine
even if I had to gouge out my eyes
How could I have believed that one day I would practice
the scorned craft of the crow
or even the dark function of the swan
Me the artisan son of the artisan
field hand of antique beauty
weaver of hope
watchman of the hearth unto ashes
shepherd without a staff
to raise against the wolf-dog
Me the artisan son of the artisan
watching out for the rainbow
to be sure of its colors
while trusting their names
gathering them up one by one
in the copper pot of my mother
like so many rare spices
meant for human pleasures
at a shared meal which becomes legitimate
only if the poor bless and honor it?

How could I have believed
that this dream which converted me to humanity
would become a nightmare
that the heroes of my youth
would cut down the tree of my song
that the books where I had met my doubles
would yellow in the depths of my library
that my wandering path toward others
would be so bereft of a cup of water
and bread left by the roadside
by He or She who watches over the wanderer?

How could I have believed
in the mirage of such a beautiful path
in the chains of such a fabulous horizon
in the worm in such a beautiful fruit
So where was the fault?

Pourquoi ce silence mon aimée
veux-tu attiser encore plus en moi la parole
me faire vaticiner, blasphémer
refaire avec les mots ce que les hommes
ont défait avec les mots
retrouver sens à ce qui s'est ligué contre le sens
arrêter d'un cri l'engrenage qui a pris tout mon corps
et ne m'a laissé que ce semblant de voix
Mais qui parle en moi
Est-ce toi, ô mon œil
ou ma parole en deuil ?
Alors va, parole
délie-moi
délire-moi
rends à ma langue ses langues perdues
ses antiques croyances
les frelons ingouvernables de ses mots
ses jungles et leurs réducteurs de têtes froides
Délivre-moi de l'étau de toute raison
Prends mes peaux de loup et d'agneau
mon encrier fossile, mes crayons
le pain des funérailles sur lequel j'ai prêté serment
Prends tout ce que j'ai écrit et remplis-en ma tombe
puissent asticots et serpents y trouver leur bonheur
Prends ce bâton de pèlerin
qui a cru guider un aveugle
Prends la dernière cigarette et jette le paquet

Va ma parole
délie-moi
délire-moi
sois drue, âpre, rêche, ardue, hérissée
Monte et bouillonne
Déverse-toi
Lave les mots traînés dans la boue
et les bouches putrides
Fais qu'en toi la vague se soulève
et d'un bond inexplicable quitte la mer
avec tous les poissons qui refusent la fatalité aquatique
Fais qu'en toi un autre magma se forme
d'un limon aguerri
et qu'il nous promette une genèse têtue

Why are you silent, my beloved
do you want to fan the flames of words in me
to make me prophesy, blaspheme
do again with words what men
have undone with words
discover again meaning in what has joined forces against meaning
stop with one cry the chain of events that has possessed my entire body
and has left me only with this semblance of a voice
But who is speaking within me
Is it you, oh my eye
or my voice in mourning?
Well then, go forth, voice
untie me
unleash me
give back to my tongue its lost tongues
its ancient beliefs
the uncontrollable hornets of its words
its jungles and their shrinkers of cold heads
Deliver me from the vise of all reason
Take my wolf and lamb skins
my fossil inkwell, my pencils
the funeral bread upon which I have taken my oath
Take this pilgrim's staff
which believed it guided a blind man
Take the last cigarette and throw the pack away

Go forth my voice
untie me
unleash me
be dense, keen, forbidding, hard, bristling
Rise up and boil
Spill over
Cleanse the words dragged through the muck
and the putrid mouths
Cause the wave to rise up within you
and with a baffling leap leave the sea
with all the fish who refuse the fate of water
Cause another magma to form within you
from a hardened silt
and may it promise us a stubborn genesis

sans enfer ni paradis
lente comme la caresse qui enflamme le désir

Va ma parole
ma loyale
Maintenant, corps entier
je parle
avec tous mes avortements
Vaincu, je ne me rends pas
Je vais ouvrir un grand chantier dans ma mémoire
allumer des torches avec les prunelles de mes martyrs
battre le tambour avec leurs mains
Nous allons danser la danse
des soleils qu'on nous a volés
des taureaux égorgés
et jetés avec nous dans nos cellules
des danseuses sacrées brûlées pour délit de danse

Ah ma parole
Ne laisse en jachère nul organe
arrose-les d'un suc de grossesse et de jouvence
Danse-moi
Danse-nous
Ruines ou pas ruines
chaos ou abysse
Dieu mort ou vif
danse toute
Je viens de toi à toi
pauvre et nu comme il se doit
avec une poignée de sel dans la bouche
les ongles noircis et longs
foulant les braises ardentes
dans un nuage de santal et de viscères fumants
levant l'étendard jaune et noir des femmes folles
prêtresses des trous dans la terre
Je viens à vous
ô mère et père
rejoindre le cortège et la robe
nouer ma foi à la corde de votre foi
J'apporte un bouc, des cierges décorés de Salé
trois pains de sucre
et un bouquet de menthe de Meknès

with no heaven no hell
slow as the caress which enflames desire

Go forth my voice
my faithful one
Now, with my whole body
I speak
with all my abortions
Vanquished, I do not surrender
I am going to open a vast work site in my memory
light torches with the eyes of my martyrs
beat the drum with their hands
We are going to dance the dance
of the suns stolen from us
of the bulls slaughtered
and thrown with us into our cells
of the sacred dancers burnt for the crime of dancing

Ah my voice
Let no organ lie fallow
bathe them in the essence of pregnancy and rejuvenation
Dance me
Dance us
Ruins or no ruins
chaos or abyss
God dead or alive
dance with your whole body
I come from you, to you
poor and naked as is befitting
with a fistful of salt in my mouth
fingernails blackened, long
treading on burning coals
in a cloud of sandalwood and smoking viscera
raising the yellow and black flag of mad women
priestesses of holes in the earth
I come to you
oh mother and father
to rejoin the procession and the robe
to knot my faith to the cord of your faith
I bring a goat, some candles from Salé
three sugared breads
and a bouquet of mint from Meknès

O faites-moi place
pour que je danse depuis le commencement
et que mon sang noir gicle sur le pavé
indique le chemin du sanctuaire
où nul Imam ne se cache
Ce sanctuaire oublié même de vous
Là où le rebelle échappe aux lois humaines
et peut vivre en homme libre

Ah parole
danse-moi
danse-nous
Je te confie ces corps en transe salutaire
ces tumeurs bénignes et non bénignes
ces talismans incrustés dans la peau
pour instiller la patience du roc
et rendre le sort moins vorace
Je te confie
ce cortège hésitant entre frénésie et soumission
Je te confie
tambours, crotales
et violons suborneurs
Je te confie
la bouilloire et les aiguières
le chaudron, le feu et ses serveurs
Je te confie
la vierge et les esprits qui l'habitent
son cri multiplié de fausse parturiente
ses seins aveuglants
ses hanches de bateau ailé fendant la nuit
Je te confie
ô maîtresse imprévisible
les vannes de cette nuit
afin que tu les lâches
à l'heure dite
sans faiblir
sur les ravisseurs de l'aube

Ah parole
d'où viendrais-je, sinon de toi
et où irais-je ?
Je n'ai plus que ce cheveu
pour porter mes pas d'un précipice l'autre

Oh make room for me
so I may dance from the beginning
and so my black blood may spurt onto the pavement
and show the way to the sanctuary
where no Imam is hiding
The sanctuary forgotten even by you
Where the rebel evades human laws
and can live as a free man

Ah my voice
dance me
dance us
I confide unto you these bodies in salutary trance
these tumors both benign and not benign
these talismans encrusted in the skin
to instill the patience of the rock
and render fate less voracious
I confide unto you
this procession wavering between frenzy and submission
I confide unto you
drums, rattlesnakes
and beguiling violins
I confide unto you
the kettle and the ewers
the cauldron, the fire and the ones who tend it
I confide unto you
the virgin and the spirits that inhabit her
her distended scream of false childbirth
her blinding breasts
her winged-ship hips cleaving the night
I confide unto you
o unpredictable mistress
the floodgates of this night
so that you may loosen them
at the appointed time
and not slacken
before the abductors of dawn

Ah my voice
where would I have come from, if not from you
and where would I go?
I have nothing more than this strand of hair
to bridge me from one cliff to another

rejoindre quelques étoiles amies
qui s'obstinent à briller dans la désolation du ciel
remonter les cercles d'un enfer incohérent
où d'aucuns ont cru que je me complaisais
Je n'ai plus que cet empan
d'un royaume
où je n'ai même pas droit à une tente
et dont je ne peux entendre le nom
sans avoir mal
là où aucun fil ne peut recoudre les blessures
Dois-je t'appeler patrie
pour me consoler ou me venger des patries
ou dois-je te laisser libre toi aussi
souveraine de racines, hérésies, amour
en permanence insurgée ?

Ah parole
ma redoutable
toi seule peux me bannir
quand nul tyran ne peut m'exiler
Toi seule peux seller ma monture
lui choisir mors, étriers
et l'engager dans d'effroyables pistes
où tu te complais à me faire lire comme un débutant
dans le sable, les cailloux et les traces refroidies
Toi seule, ô femme jalouse
ne peux accepter ni défaillance ni infidélité
Et voilà que tu me jettes tel un mouchoir en papier
dans ce chaos
Voilà que tu me donnes en exercice
cette fin de monde
avec pour tâche de déceler dans les décombres
la pierre noire ou blanche
la graine manquante
l'anneau de bois
ou l'organe tombé en déshérence
l'un ou l'autre de ces chaînons
qu'il faudra ajuster à l'âme
quand viendra l'ère
d'une autre vie aventureuse
Et j'obtempère
je cherche
j'ajoute mon désordre au désordre du monde

to join a few friendly stars
still stubbornly shining in the grieving sky
to reassemble the circles of a muddled hell
where some have thought I took pleasure
I have only this span
of a kingdom
where I am not even allowed a tent
and whose name I cannot hear
without feeling pain
where no thread can suture the wounds
Must I call you homeland
to console myself or avenge myself of other homelands
or must I let you go too,
sovereign of roots, heresies, love
in permanent rebellion?

Ah my voice
my fierce one
you alone can banish me
when no tyrant can exile me
You alone can saddle my mount
choose the bit, the stirrups
and urge her onto terrifying trails
where you delight in making me read like a novice
in the sand, the pebbles and the cold tracks
You alone, o jealous woman
can accept neither lapses nor faithlessness
And then you toss me aside like a rag
into this chaos
And you give me as an exercise
this end of the world
with the task of finding in the debris
the black or white stone
the missing seed
the wooden ring
or the organ escheated
one or the other of these chain-links
which must be fitted to the soul
when the age comes
of another adventurous life
And I comply
I seek
I add my confusion to the confusion of the world

J'écris pour ne pas me perdre, ne pas tomber
J'écris en regardant fiévreusement ma montre
la course du soleil
l'ombre portée sur le mur
Je cherche dans le sable pollué
le bout de bois rond
le moindre éclat de pierre blanche
Je guette les oiseaux qui se posent
pour aller leur disputer la fameuse graine
Je fouille dans mes artères sclérosées
pour trouver quelque organe
dont on ne m'a pas appris l'existence à l'école
Et puis, dis-moi
comment déceler une pierre noire dans les ténèbres ?

J'écris avec le tout et le rien
l'énergie du désespoir
et Dieu sait si elle est grande
Je travaille aussi dur qu'un pauvre maçon
que le sort a désigné pour construire des villas de riches
qu'un mineur qui s'acharne sur le ventre de la terre
pour se venger de sa stérilité
qu'il reproche bien sûr à sa femme

J'écris comme d'autres prient
font pénitence
et acceptent le Mystère
J'ai parfois des joies comme eux
des éblouissements
mais j'ai souvent des doutes qu'ils ignorent
des tourments qui donnent à ma prière
ses accents de vérité défiant la foi

J'écris
quand tu m'écris
ô parole
et j'ajoute des choses qui t'échappent
quand je soumets tes mots à l'ordalie
réveille en eux la mémoire qui te précède
Quand je cesse de les traiter comme des esclaves
et les caresse dans le sens de la dignité
Quand je leur donne des rendez-vous amoureux
et arrive avant l'heure pour déguster mon attente

I write so as not to lose my way, not to fall
I write while feverishly checking my watch
the course of the sun
the shadow cast upon the wall
I search in the polluted sand for
the round of wood
the least sparkle of white stone
I watch out for the birds that alight
to compete with them for the celebrated seed
I search my arteries
to find some organ
I never learned of at school
And then, tell me
how to find a black stone in the darkness?

I write with everything and with nothing
the energy of despair
and God knows how great it is
I work as hard as a poor mason
whom destiny has chosen to build villas for the rich
as a miner who keeps clawing at the earth's womb
to take his revenge on his sterility
which he naturally blames on his wife

I write as others pray
do penitence
and accept the Mystery
I sometimes have joys like them
amazements
yet I often have doubts unknown to them
torments which lend to my prayer
its accents of truth defying faith

I write
when you write me
O voice
and I add things which elude you
when I submit your words to the ordeal
awaken in them the memory that precedes you
When I stop treating them like slaves
and caress their dignity
When I set a time to meet with them as lovers
and arrive early to savor my wait

Quand je les invite après le verre de courtoisie
à un repas où nous mangeons avec les doigts
dans le même plat
quand je n'exige rien d'eux
hormis ce que nous devons
à notre souveraine liberté

J'écris par compassion
en tendant ma sébile
et peu importe si je n'y récolte que des crachats

Ah parole
vois comme tu m'as endurci
Je suis devenu ton enclume
Les marteaux du monde peuvent frapper
je ne me courberai pas
J'attendrai qu'ils s'épuisent
pour me préparer au monde suivant
Et qu'il prépare lui aussi ses marteaux !

Ai-je dormi, mon amour
Qu'ai-je dit de ce que j'ai cru voir
D'où vient ce cheveu
que j'ai, noué autour de la langue
Pourquoi suis-je tout courbatu ?
Mes pieds sont enflés
Ma tête s'est comme vidée d'une eau lourde
Mais je me sens apaisé
prêt à voir et à entendre
me dégager de ton étreinte
et me présenter devant la Balance
pour peser mon âme
ce que mes deux paumes ont pu posséder
y déposer les quelques plumes qui restent de mes ailes
le mouchoir brodé que j'ai oublié dans ma poche
Je ne garderai sur moi que notre bague commune
Ni l'ange du bien ni l'ange du mal ne me la prendra
Je la défendrai avec mes dents et mes ongles
ma rage de grand handicapé
Je la garderai
et comme dans les vieux contes
je la ferai tourner
quand le geôlier aura cru fermer toutes les issues

When I invite them after a welcoming drink
to a meal where we eat with our fingers
from the same dish
when I demand nothing from them
beyond what we owe
to our sovereign liberty

I write with compassion
while holding out my beggar's cup
and it matters little if I collect nothing but spit

Ah my voice
see how you have hardened me
I have become your anvil
The hammers of the world can strike
I will not bend
I will wait until they become weary
in order to ready myself for the next world
And let it too prepare its hammers!

Have I slept, my love
What did I say of what I thought I saw
Where does this strand of hair come from
tied around my tongue
Why am I stiff all over?
My feet are swollen
My head seems emptied of a heavy water
But I feel calmed
ready to see and to hear
to disengage myself from your embrace
and to present myself before the Scales
to weigh my soul
what my two palms have been able to possess
to place there the few feathers that remain of my wings
the embroidered handkerchief I forgot in my pocket
I will only keep our shared ring
Neither the angel of good nor the angel of evil will take it from me
I will defend it with my teeth and my nails
with the rage of my terrible handicap
I will keep it
and as in the old tales
I will make it turn
when the jailer thinks he has locked all the doors

Il y aura un grondement et une tour de fumée
un tremblement et un vol impromptu de perdrix
Et le miracle sera là
nos pouls qui battent paisiblement
jouent leur symphonie
poignet contre poignet
pendant que nous voguons
sur l'empan de notre île
avec une nouvelle provision de mots
un peu d'eau douce
quelques fruits
en sachant que notre esquif est de ce monde
qui s'écroule autour de nous
en nous
Notre esquif est de ce monde
encore plus perdu que nous
Notre esquif est de ce monde
éberlué
trop jeune ou trop vieux
pour comprendre
qu'une petite bague
peut faire un miracle

Créteil, mars 1992

There will be an angry murmur and a tower of smoke
a trembling and the unexpected flight of a partridge
And the miracle will be there
our pulses peacefully beating
playing their symphony
wrist against wrist
while we are sailing
on the span of our island
with a new supply of words
a little fresh water
some fruit
knowing that our skiff is of this world
crumbling around us
within us
Our skiff is of this world
more lost even than we
Our skiff is of this world
struck dumb
too young or too old
to understand
that a tiny ring
can craft a miracle

Créteil, March 1992

UNE SEULE MAIN NE SUFFIT PAS POUR ÉCRIRE

LE PAYS S'ÉLOIGNE MAINTENANT

Le pays s'éloigne maintenant
avec ses mouettes orphelines
et sa lourde porte
Il y a
en guise d'aube
une ombre et son sarcasme
L'homme sans tête
court dans le labyrinthe
avec ce qui lui reste de cœur
Dans sa main
il tient l'inutile
une clé souillée
par la guerre et ses mensonges
L'œil
exilé de sa lumière
s'épanche sur le sable

LES RÊVES VIENNENT MOURIR SUR LA PAGE

Un à un
les rêves viennent mourir sur la page
Ils se sont donné le mot
ils viennent de partout
pour mourir sur la page
comme les éléphants dans leur cimetière
J'assiste à leurs convulsions
ne peux tendre un verre d'eau
Je les regarde pour la première fois
pour la dernière fois
avant de les envelopper dans le suaire de mes mots
et les déposer sur la barque menue
qui fut jadis leur berceau
Le courant les emporte
et bien vite me les ramène
comme si le large n'était pas là-bas
mais ici sur la page

WRITING REQUIRES MORE THAN ONE HAND

Now the country grows distant

Now the country grows distant
with its orphan seagulls
and its heavy gate
There is
disguised as dawn
a taunting shadow
The headless man
is running through the labyrinth
with what heart remains to him
In his hand
he clutches what is useless
a key defiled
by the war and its lies
The eye
exiled from its light
splays over the sand

Dreams come to die upon the page

One by one
dreams come to die upon the page
They passed the word on
they come from everywhere
to die upon the page
like elephants in their graveyard
I witness their convulsions
am unable to offer them a cup of water
I look at them for the first time
for the last time
before wrapping them in the shroud of my words
and setting them on the tiny craft
which was once their cradle
The current carries them away
and brings them back to me quickly
as if the open sea were not out there
but here upon the page

JE SUIS L'ENFANT DE CE SIÈCLE

Je suis l'enfant de ce siècle pitoyable
l'enfant qui n'a pas grandi
Les questions qui me brûlaient la langue
ont brûlé mes ailes
J'avais appris à marcher
puis j'ai désappris
Je me suis lassé des oasis
et des chamelles avides de ruines
Etendu au milieu du chemin
la tête tournée vers l'Orient
j'attends la caravane des fous

ILE

Cette île
loin des mots
qui ne savent que blesser
plantés dans la langue
comme des barreaux
Cette île
loin du corps
qui ne sait que désirer
exsangue
et invaincu
Cette île
où naît le silence
bercé par la comptine
d'avant la mort douce
Ile
de nulle part
papillon de sang
lâché dans l'éternité

J'OSE PARLER DE MES TÉNÈBRES

J'ose parler de mes ténèbres
Je suis dans les ténèbres
et n'implore ni planche ni salut
Je vais habiter ce chaos
le meubler comme on meuble une cellule
me faire une couche avec la paille de mes livres

I AM A CHILD OF THIS CENTURY

I am a child of this pitiful century
the child who didn't grow up
The questions that once burned my tongue
have burned my wings
I had learned to walk
then I unlearned
I grew weary of oases
and camels thirsting for ruins
Stretched out in the middle of the road
my head turned toward the Orient
I am waiting for the caravan of madmen

ISLAND

This island
far from words
which can only hurt
rooted in the tongue
like bars
This island
far from the body
which knows only desire
bloodless
and untamed
This island
where silence is born
rocked by a lullaby
from before sweet death
Island
of nowhere
butterfly of blood
released into eternity

I RISK SPEAKING OF MY DARKNESS

I risk speaking of my darkness
I am wrapped in darkness
and do not beg for deliverance
I will live inside this chaos
furnish it like a cell
make a bed with the straw of my books

me ligoter les mains
pour ne pas succomber à la tentation
tailler avec ma flamme noire
une fenêtre dans le mur de la nuit
Je vivrai, veillerai ainsi
épouvantail dressé
dans le champ des ténèbres

LE DÉSESPOIR, C'EST MON ENFANT

Ne vous réjouissez pas trop vite de mon désespoir
Le désespoir
c'est mon enfant handicapé
Il me raconte avec ses yeux
l'histoire de la hache d'amour
Ses doigts crochus sont ma boussole
je les embrasse et ne les compte pas
Sa douleur est ma source
Sa soif me fait inventer l'eau
La nourriture que je porte à sa bouche
il faut que je l'arrache de ma chair
Le désespoir
c'est mon enfant handicapé
Il me tient éveillé
et somme toute m'aide à marcher
aussi bien que la canne de l'espoir

IL Y A UN CANNIBALE QUI ME LIT

Il y a un cannibale qui me lit
C'est un lecteur férocement intelligent
un lecteur de rêve
Il ne laisse passer aucun mot
sans en soupeser le poids de sang
Il soulève même les virgules
pour découvrir les morceaux de choix
Il sait lui que la page vibre
d'une splendide respiration
Ah cet émoi qui rend la proie
alléchante et déjà soumise
Il attend la fatigue
qui descend sur le visage
comme un masque de sacrifice

bind my hands
to avoid temptation
and with my black flame carve
a window in the wall of night
Thus will I live, keep watch
a scarecrow standing
in the field of darkness

DESPAIR IS MY CHILD

Don't rejoice too quickly at my despair
Despair
is my handicapped child
He tells me with his eyes
the story of love's hatchet
His crooked fingers are my compass
I kiss them and don't count them
His pain is my spring
His thirst makes me invent water
The food I lift to his mouth
I must tear from my flesh
Despair
is my handicapped child
He keeps me awake
and in the end helps me walk
as much as the cane of hope

THERE IS A CANNIBAL READING ME

There is a cannibal reading me
A fiercely intelligent reader
a dream reader
He doesn't let a word go by
without measuring its weight in blood
He even stirs up the commas
to find the tasty bits
He knows that the page vibrates
with a splendid breathing
Ah the frenzy that makes the prey
enticing and submissive
He waits for a sign of fatigue
to shadow my face
like a sacrificial mask

Il cherche la faille pour bondir
l'adjectif de trop
la répétition qui ne pardonne pas
Il y a un cannibale qui me lit
pour se nourrir

LA LANGUE DE MA MÈRE

Je n'ai pas vu ma mère depuis vingt ans
Elle s'est laissée mourir de faim
On raconte qu'elle enlevait chaque matin son foulard de tête
et frappait sept fois le sol
en maudissant le ciel et le Tyran
J'étais dans la caverne
là où le forçat lit dans les ombres
et peint sur les parois le bestiaire de l'avenir
Je n'ai pas vu ma mère depuis vingt ans
Elle m'a laissé un service à café chinois
dont les tasses se cassent une à une
sans que je les regrette tant elles sont laides
Mais je n'en aime que plus le café
Aujourd'hui, quand je suis seul
j'emprunte la voix de ma mère
ou plutôt c'est elle qui parle dans ma bouche
avec ses jurons, ses grossièretés et ses imprécations
le chapelet introuvable de ses diminutifs
toute l'espèce menacée de ses mots
Je n'ai pas vu ma mère depuis vingt ans
mais je suis le dernier homme
à parler encore sa langue

LE MERLE

Merle
pourquoi viens-tu te poser sur mon unique branche ?
Merle
éloigne-toi
Laisse-moi vivre ma vie d'oiseau
sur mon unique branche
lui rappeler sa promesse de bourgeons
et lui verser ce qui me reste de sève
Merle

He seeks the weak spot
before pouncing:
the superfluous adjective
the inexcusable repetition
There is a cannibal who reads me
to feed himself

MY MOTHER'S LANGUAGE

I haven't seen my mother for twenty years
She let herself starve to death
They say she removed her scarf each morning
and struck the earth seven times
cursing the sky and the Tyrant
I was in the cave
where the convict reads in the shadows
and paints on the walls the bestiary of the future
I haven't seen my mother for twenty years
She left me a Chinese coffee set
one by one the cups break and
I don't miss them, they are so ugly
But I love the coffee in them all the more
Today, when I am alone
I borrow my mother's voice
or rather she speaks in my mouth
with her curses, her profanities and invectives
the rare rosary of her pet names
all the endangered species of her words
I have not seen my mother for twenty years
but I am the last man
who still speaks her language

THE BLACKBIRD

Blackbird
why do you come and land upon my only branch?
Blackbird
go away
Let me live my bird's life
upon my only branch
reminding it of its promise to bloom
and spill what is left of my sap
Blackbird

pourquoi viens-tu picorer mon dernier fruit ?
Merle
éloigne-toi
Laisse-moi ce souvenir de la saison affolante
où je chantais pour la Création entière
et trouvais ma voix belle
Merle
pourquoi me prends-tu ma branche
mon illusion de branche
et me condamnes-tu aux éternels barreaux ?

UNE SEULE MAIN NE SUFFIT PAS POUR ÉCRIRE

Une seule main ne suffit pas pour écrire
Par les temps qui courent
il en faudrait deux
Et que la deuxième apprenne vite
les métiers de l'indicible :
broder le nom de l'étoile
qui se lèvera après la prochaine apocalypse
reconnaître entre mille le fil qui ne casse pas
coudre dans l'étoffe des passions
langes, capes et linceuls
sculpter l'aube dans un tas d'immondices
Deux mains ne suffisent pas pour écrire
Par les temps qui courent
et les misères qui grondent
il en faudrait trois, quatre
pour que la vie daigne visiter
ce terrible désert blanc

LES LOUPS

J'entends les loups
Ils sont bien au chaud dans leurs maisons de campagne
Ils regardent goulûment la télévision
Pendant des heures, ils comptent à voix haute les cadavres
et chantent à tue-tête des airs de réclame
Je vois les loups
Ils mangent à treize le gibier du jour
élisent à main levée le Judas de service
Pendant des heures, ils boivent un sang de village

why do you come and peck at my last fruit?
Blackbird
go away
Leave me the memory of the delirious season
when I sang for all of Creation
and found my voice beautiful
Blackbird
why are you taking my branch
my illusion of a branch
and condemning me to eternal bars?

WRITING REQUIRES MORE THAN ONE HAND

Writing requires more than one hand
With things as they are
two would be needed
And the second one would need to learn quickly
the crafts of the ineffable:
to embroider the name of the star
that will rise after the next apocalypse
to recognize among thousands the thread that will not break
to sew into the fabric of passions
swaddling cloths, capes and shrouds
to sculpt dawn in a mound of filth
Writing requires more than two hands
With things as they are
and the snarling miseries
three, four would be needed
so that life might deign to visit
this terrible white desert

THE WOLVES

I hear the wolves
They are cozy in their country houses
They greedily watch television
For hours, they count the corpses out loud
and loudly sing the tunes of commercials
I see the wolves
Thirteen of them are eating the prey of the day
and with a show of hands elect
the Judas on duty
For hours, they drink a local blood

encore jeune, peu fruité
à la robe défaite
le sang d'une terre où sommeillent des charniers
J'entends les loups
Ils éteignent à minuit
et violent légalement leurs femmes

EN VAIN J'ÉMIGRE

J'émigre en vain
Dans chaque ville je bois le même café
et me résigne au visage fermé du serveur
Les rires de mes voisins de table
taraudent la musique du soir
Une femme passe pour la dernière fois
En vain j'émigre
et m'assure de mon éloignement
Dans chaque ciel je retrouve un croissant de lune
et le silence têtu des étoiles
Je parle en dormant
un mélange de langues
et de cris d'animaux
La chambre où je me réveille
est celle où je suis né
J'émigre en vain
Le secret des oiseaux m'échappe
comme celui de cet aimant
qui affole à chaque étape
ma valise

DEUX HEURES DE TRAIN

En deux heures de train
je repasse le film de ma vie
Deux minutes par année en moyenne
Une demi-heure pour l'enfance
une autre pour la prison
L'amour, les livres, l'errance
se partagent le reste
La main de ma compagne

still young, not very fruity
dull color
the blood of a land where mass graves
lay in troubled sleep
I hear the wolves
They turn off their lights at midnight
and legally rape their wives

I EMIGRATE IN VAIN

I emigrate in vain
In each city I drink the same coffee
endure the waiter's closed face
The laughter from the adjacent table
pierces the evening music
A woman passes by one last time
It's vain to emigrate
and ensure my distance
In each sky I find a crescent moon
and the stubborn silence of stars
Asleep I speak
a jumble of languages
and animal cries
I awaken in the room
where I was born
I emigrate in vain
The secret of birds eludes me
like the secret of that magnet
that at every stop
spins the needle
of the compass in
my suitcase

TWO HOURS ON THE TRAIN

In two hours on the train
I replay the film of my life
Two minutes per year, on average
A half hour for childhood
another for prison
Love, books, wandering
take up the rest
The hand of my companion

fond peu à peu dans la mienne
et sa tête sur mon épaule
est aussi légère qu'une colombe
A notre arrivée
j'aurai la cinquantaine
et il me restera à vivre
une heure environ

LES MIETTES SOUS LA TABLE

Je rends leur noblesse
à ces miettes sous la table
Je me baisse humblement
les ramasse, les embrasse une à une
et les dépose dans la haute fissure
O mur qui menaces ruine
Hirondelles averties
qui déménagez déjà vos nids
O monde échoué comme un superbe voilier
voici ces miettes rendues à leur noblesse
Je les dépose dans la haute fissure
et dis : Ceci est mon esprit
ramassé sous la table

UNE MAISON LÀ-BAS

Une maison là-bas
avec sa porte ouverte
et ses deux tourterelles
récitant inlassablement le nom de l'absent
Une maison là-bas
avec son puits profond
et sa terrasse aussi blanche
que le sel des constellations
Une maison là-bas
pour que l'errant se dise
j'ai lieu d'errer
tant qu'il y aura une maison là-bas

slowly melts into my own
and her head on my shoulder
is light as a dove
When we arrive
I'll be fifty
and I'll have
about an hour to live

CRUMBS UNDER THE TABLE

To these crumbs beneath the table
I give back their dignity
Humbly I bend down
gather them up, kiss them one by one
and place them in this high crack
O wall threatening to collapse
Swallows forewarned
already moving your nests away
O world run aground like a superb sailing ship
here are these crumbs restored to their dignity
I place them in the high crack
and I say: This is my spirit
gathered from beneath the table

A HOUSE OVER THERE

A house over there
with its open door
and its two turtle doves
reciting tirelessly
the name of the missing one
A house over there
with its deep well
and its terrace as white
as the salt of constellations
A house over there
so that the wanderer might say
I have reason to wander
as long as there is a house
over there

LE NOM

Peu à peu ton nom s'efface
et tu te dis : C'est bien
Tu accroches ta charrue à la seule étoile
qui ne te mettra pas la corde au cou
Tu la pousses et elle te pousse
dans la cohue du ciel
où la loi est fille du pur désir
et tu te dis : C'est bien
Tu n'es plus en mesure d'exiger
des droits sur la mémoire
Tu la sais frivole
soumise au glaive
Tu creuses un sillon autre
dans la terre ingrate
qui n'attise nulle convoitise
et tu te dis : C'est ainsi
Ni bien ni mal
Chacun sa petite croix
le mur sur lequel il crachera sa folie
Peu à peu ton nom s'efface
Celui-là que tu n'as pas choisi
Bientôt ce sera la fête du Sacrifice
Tu achèteras un mouton et tu l'égorgeras
en prononçant à l'envers
les lettres du nom oublié

ABRÉGÉ D'ÉTERNITÉ

Sur le radeau, j'allumerai un cierge
et j'inventerai ma prière
Je laisserai à la vague inspirée
le soin d'ériger son temple
Je revêtirai de ma cape
le premier poisson
qui viendra se frotter à mes rames
J'irai ainsi par nuit et par mer
sans vivres ni mouettes
avec un bout de cierge
et un brin de prière
J'irai ainsi

THE NAME

Little by little your name fades
and you tell yourself: That's fine
You hitch your plough to the only star
that will not tie the rope around your neck
You push it and it pushes you
in the crowded sky
where the law is born of pure desire
and you tell yourself: That's fine
You are no longer in a position
to make demands on your memory
You know it is frivolous
subject to the sword
You plow another furrow
in the barren earth
which arouses no envy
and you tell yourself: That's the way it is
Neither good nor bad
To each one his little cross
the wall upon which he will spit out his madness
Little by little, your name fades
The one you did not choose
Soon it will be the feast of Sacrifice
You will buy a sheep and you will cut its throat
saying the letters of
the forgotten name
backwards

SYNOPSIS OF ETERNITY

On the raft, I will light a candle
and I will invent my prayer
I will leave to the inspired wave
the task of building its temple
I will cover with my cape
the first fish
that rubs against my oars
Thus I will go by night and by sea
with no food nor seagulls
with a stub of candle
and a wisp of prayer
Thus will I go

avec mon visage d'illuminé
et je me dirai
ô moitié d'homme, réjouis-toi
tu vivras si tu ne l'as déjà vécu
un abrégé d'éternité

LA VIE

La vie
Il me suffit de m'être réveillé
le soleil dans ma droite
la lune dans ma gauche
et d'avoir marché
depuis le ventre de ma mère
jusqu'au crépuscule de ce siècle
La vie
Il me suffit d'avoir goûté à ce fruit
J'ai vu ce que j'ai dit
je n'ai rien tu de l'horreur
j'ai fait ce que j'ai pu
j'ai tout pris et donné à l'amour
La vie
Ni plus ni moins que ce miracle
sans témoins
Ah corps meurtri
âme meurtrie
Avouez un peu votre bonheur
Avouez-le
rien qu'entre nous

with my visionary face
and I will say to myself
O half of a man, rejoice
you will know
if you have not yet known
a synopsis of eternity

LIFE

Life
It is enough to have awakened
the sun in my right hand
the moon in my left
and to have walked
from my mother's womb
to the twilight of this century
Life
It is enough to have tasted this fruit
I have seen what I have said
I have hidden nothing of the horror
I have done what I could
I have taken everything from love
given everything to love
Life
No more no less than this miracle
unwitnessed
Ah bruised body
wounded soul
Admit your happiness
Admit it
just between us

Le Spleen de Casablanca

LE SPLEEN DE CASABLANCA

la mémoire de mon père

Dans le bruit d'une ville sans âme
j'apprends le dur métier du retour
Dans ma poche crevée
je n'ai que ta main
pour réchauffer la mienne
tant l'été se confond avec l'hiver
Où s'en est allé, dis-moi
le pays de notre jeunesse ?

O comme les pays se ressemblent
et se ressemblent les exils
Tes pas ne sont pas de ces pas
qui laissent des traces sur le sable
Tu passes sans passer

Visage après visage
meurent les ans
Je cherche dans les yeux une lueur
un bourgeon dans les paroles
Et j'ai peur, très peur
de perdre encore un vieil ami

The Spleen of Casablanca

THE SPLEEN OF CASABLANCA

To the memory of my father

In the noise of a soulless city
I learn the tough trade of return
In my torn pocket
I have only your hand
to warm mine
so like winter has summer become
Where has it gone, tell me
the country of our youth?

O how alike the countries
and how alike the exiles
Your steps are not like those
that leave marks on the sand
You pass by and you don't

Face after face
the years vanish
I look for a glimmer in eyes
a blossom in words
And I am afraid, very afraid
of losing one more old friend

Ce gris matin est loyal
Je lui sais gré du spleen qu'il répand
de la douleur qu'il recueille
de la gerbe des doutes qu'il m'offre
en bon connaisseur

Si je sors
où irai-je ?
Les trottoirs sont défoncés
Les arbres font pitié
Les immeubles cachent le ciel
Les voitures règnent
comme n'importe quel tyran
Les cafés sont réservés aux hommes
Les femmes, à raison
ont peur qu'on les regarde
Et puis
je n'ai de rendez-vous
avec personne

Je ne suis pas ce nomade
qui cherche le puits
que le sédentaire a creusé
Je bois peu d'eau
et marche
à l'écart de la caravane

Le siècle prend fin
dit-on
et cela me laisse indifférent
Quoique le suivant
ne me dise rien qui vaille

Dans la cité de ciment et de sel
ma grotte est en papier

This grey morning is loyal
I am grateful for the spleen it diffuses
the pain it gathers
the sheaf of doubts it offers me
as a perfect connoisseur

If I go out
where will I go?
The sidewalks are dilapidated
The trees are pitiful
The buildings hide the sky
Cars rule
like a common tyrant
Cafés are reserved for men
Women, for good reason
are afraid of being looked at
And then
I have a rendezvous
with no one.

I am not that nomad
looking for the well
the sedentary drilled
I drink little water
and walk
apart from the caravan

The century is ending
they say
and I am indifferent
Though the next one
doesn't fill me with delight

In the city of cement and salt
my cave is made of paper

J'ai une bonne provision de plumes
et de quoi faire du café
Mes idées n'ont pas d'ombre
pas plus d'odeur
Mon corps a disparu
Il n'y a plus que ma tête
dans cette grotte en papier

J'essaye de vivre
La tâche est ardue

Quel sens donner à ce voyage
Quelle autre langue
me faudra-t-il apprendre
Lequel de mes doigts
devrai-je sacrifier
Et si mes lèvres repoussent
saurai-je encore embrasser ?

Je frapperai
à toutes les portes de la ville
et je crierai :
Je suis étranger

Le froid
s'est installé
à la source

Mère
je t'appelle
alors que tu n'es plus que poussière
Il faut que je te dise :
Je suis ton éternel enfant

I have a good stock of pens
and what I need to make coffee
My ideas have neither shadow
nor odor
My body has disappeared
My head is all that is left
in this paper cave

I am trying to live
The task is arduous

What meaning should I give to this journey
What other language
shall I have to learn
Which of my fingers
must I sacrifice
And if my lips grow back
will I still know how to kiss?

I will knock
at all the gates of the city
and I will cry out:
I am a stranger

The cold
has taken hold
at the source.

Mother
I am calling you
though you are only dust now
I must tell you this:
I am your eternal child

Grandir
est au-dessus de mes forces

Poète
réjouis-toi de ces questions
qui te réveillent
au milieu de la nuit
et ne pâlissent pas à l'aube
avec les étoiles

Cette nuit
je me suis encore réveillé
Nulle question ne s'est présentée
J'ai ouvert un livre
et c'est comme si j'avais ouvert
une antique blessure
Hé toi l'amoureux, m'écriai-je
comment peux-tu ainsi
te sentir seul au monde ?

Les grandes feuilles m'intimident
Je les coupe en deux
pour écrire
des demi-poèmes

Les mots que j'aime
m'aiment-ils
Si je les égrène
que me restera-t-il à dire ?

Verre après verre
nous réveillons la vie

Growing up
is too much for me

Poet
rejoice in these questions
that wake you up
in the middle of the night
and do not fade at dawn
with the stars

Last night
I woke up again
No question came to me
I opened a book
and it was as if I had opened
an ancient wound
Hey you, the lover, I cried out
how can you feel
so alone in the world?

The large sheets of paper
intimidate me
I cut them in two
to write
half-poems

The words I like
do they like me?
If I shell them
what will I have left to say?

Glass after glass
we awaken life

Elle ouvre un œil
nous sourit vaguement
et se rendort

Ce que j'ai fait
je le dois à ma solitude
et à la solitude des autres
Mieux que la rencontre
il y a son attente

Le soleil est là
Je n'ai plus à l'acheter
Et bien vite je l'oublie
comme si j'étais fasciné
par les ténèbres

Les pays
maintenant
se valent
en férocité

Après les actes vains
les paroles vaines
donnant la nostalgie des actes

Les livres qui portent mon nom
et que je n'ose ouvrir
de peur
qu'ils ne tombent en poussière
entre mes doigts

It opens one eye
smiles at us vaguely
and falls back to sleep

What I have done
I owe to my solitude
and to the solitude of the others
Better than the encounter
the anticipation

The sun is here
I no longer have to buy it
And very quickly I forget it
as though I were dazzled
by darkness

Countries
now
equal each other
in ferocity

After vain deeds
vain words
leaving a yearning
for deeds

The books that bear my name
and which I dare not open
for fear
they will crumble to dust
between my fingers

A force de côtoyer le monstre
l'odeur du monstre
te colle à la peau

Réveille-toi
rebelle
Le monde croule
sous les apparences
Il va crever
de résignation

Quand j'avais froid
et faim
(j'ai connu cela
ne vous en déplaise)
la vie m'était presque douce
et fécondes mes insomnies
Je pensais chaque nuit aux autres
(aux laissés-pour-compte
ne vous en déplaise)
et chaque matin
un soleil fraternel
venait me rendre visite
et déposait à mon chevet
deux ou trois
morceaux de sucre

J'ai besoin d'un répit
le temps que vous voudrez bien m'accorder
pour ouvrir une fenêtre
sur un temps que je n'ai pas encore visité
une île de chair princière
qui s'offrira à moi pour de bon
Je pousserai cette fenêtre bleue
et je ferai vite avant qu'elle ne se referme
Je ne dirai pas ce que j'aurai vu

Keep rubbing shoulders
with the monster
and the odor of the monster
sticks to your skin

Wake up
rebel
The world is crumbling
beneath appearances
It is going to croak of
abdication

When I was cold
and hungry
(I have known that
whatever you may think)
life was almost sweet
and my insomnia fertile
Every night I would think of the others
(the misfits
whatever you think)
and every morning
a fraternal sun
would visit me
and leave at my bedside
two or three
lumps of sugar

I need a break
the time that you would kindly spare me
to open a window
onto a time I have not yet visited
an island of princely flesh
which will offer itself to me in earnest
I will push this blue window open
and I will hurry before it closes again
I will not say what I see there

Ce que j'aurai éprouvé
ira rejoindre le mystère
Si seulement vous m'accordiez ce répit
M'est avis que je vous rendrais
friands d'énigmes

Le poète invente une rose
mais ne sait quelle couleur lui donner
Comment est-ce la couleur du secret ?
Tiédeur reconnaissable au creux de l'oreille
Visage rayonnant du père
emporté par la mort douce
Ride naissante au flanc de l'aimée ?
Rien de cela ne définit une couleur
L'invention de notre poète
restera donc incomplète

J'avais une source
et j'étais économe de son eau
Je croyais fermement au partage
et ne pouvais soupçonner d'inconstance
ma source
Jusqu'au jour où elle s'est détournée de moi
prodiguant à d'autres ses bontés
Faut-il épuiser ce que l'on aime
afin de le garder ?

Il paraît que la porte de l'enfer
avoisine celle du paradis
Le grand menuisier les a conçues
dans le même bois vulgaire
Le peintre manitou les a barbouillées
de la même couleur
Comment les distinguer dans cette pénombre ?
Voyons
As-tu les clés

What I experience there
will merge with the mystery
If you just allowed me this break
It seems to me I would make you
fond of enigmas.

The poet invents a rose
but does not know what color to give it
What is the color of the secret?
Discernable warmth in the hollow of an ear
Radiant face of the father
carried away by sweet death
A new wrinkle on the beloved's breast?
None of this defines a color
Our poet's invention
will hence remain incomplete

I used to have a spring
and I was sparing of its water
I firmly believed in sharing
and could not suspect my spring
of fickleness
Until the day it turned away from me
lavishing its kindnesses on others
Must we use up what we love
to keep it for ourselves?

They say that the gate of hell
is next to the gate of paradise
The great carpenter carved them
from the same common wood
The divine painter daubed them
with the same color
How can you tell them apart
in this darkness?
Let's see
Do you have the keys

Quelle est la bonne
Et puis pourquoi te risquerais-tu
à ouvrir
ce qui ne pourrait donner
que sur le néant ?

La nuit
un semblant de pays
s'absente de lui-même
Il sort ses mandibules
pour happer les images sulfureuses
des galaxies promises
Il boit mange et se masturbe
aux frais de la princesse
Et quand à l'aube
le muezzin appelle à la prière
il se met à ronfler
comme n'importe quel mécréant

Je tire les rideaux
pour pouvoir fumer à ma guise
Je tire les rideaux
pour boire un verre
à la santé d'Abou Nouwas
Je tire les rideaux
pour lire le dernier livre de Rushdie
Bientôt, qui sait
il faudra que je descende à la cave
et que je m'enferme à double tour
pour pouvoir
penser
à ma guise

Les gardiens sont partout
Ils règnent sur les poubelles
les garages
les boîtes aux lettres
Les gardiens sont partout

Which one fits
And why would you risk
opening
what could only lead
into nothingness?

At night
a semblance of a country
goes away by itself
It spreads its jaws
to snap up sulfurous images
of promised galaxies
It drinks eats and masturbates
at the government's expense
And when at dawn
the muezzin calls the faithful to prayer
it starts snoring
like any other unbeliever

I pull the curtains
to smoke as I please
I pull the curtains
to have a drink
to the health of Abou Nouwas
I pull the curtains
to read the latest Rushdie book
Soon, who knows
I may have to go down to the cellar
and double-lock myself in
to be able
to think
as I please

The guards are everywhere
They rule over the garbage cans
over the garages
over the mail boxes
The guards are everywhere

dans les bouteilles vides
sous la langue
derrière les miroirs
Les gardiens sont partout
entre la chair et l'ongle
les narines et la rose
l'œil et le regard
Les gardiens sont partout
dans la poussière qu'on avale
et le morceau qu'on recrache
Les gardiens croissent et se multiplient
A ce rythme
arrivera le jour
où nous deviendrons tous
un peuple de gardiens

Une ville
ou sa fiction
Un peuple
ou sa rumeur ?
Là, devant l'amphithéâtre
que la mer a sculpté
un cheval blessé
superbement harnaché
implore le coup de grâce
Nous sommes dans une réception mondaine
et les convives
y compris les anciens guérilleros
ont dû déposer leurs armes
au vestiaire

Que vois-tu dans le noir ?
Regarde bien
Considère plutôt que le noir
est une couleur
comme le jaune
ou le lilas
Imagine que c'est la main d'un peintre

in the empty bottles
under your tongue
behind the mirrors
The guards are everywhere
between the flesh and the fingernail
the nostrils and the rose
the eye and the gaze
The guards are everywhere
in the dust you swallow
and the piece you spit out
The guards are increasing
multiplying
At this rate
the day will come
when we'll all become
a nation of guards

A city
or its fiction
A people
or its rumor?
There, in front of the amphitheater
that the sea sculpted
a wounded horse
superbly harnessed
begs for the coup de grâce
We are at a fashionable reception
and the guests
including the former guerrillas
had to leave their weapons
in the cloakroom

What do you see in the dark?
Look hard
Consider rather that black
is a color
like yellow
or lilac
Imagine that it was the hand of a painter

qui l'a étalée
puis s'est retirée de la toile
Epouse son mouvement
Et maintenant
réalises-tu que c'est le noir
qui voit en toi ?

Le vertige se met en place
Le désordre pousse ses vagues
Le chaos a des couleurs
un œil
Les amants halètent
sur un lit de glaise et de canicule
Une pomme n'arrête pas de tomber
Un nom est donné à l'eau
puis au feu
La Création hésite
entre l'arme absolue
et le plus bel agneau du monde
Qui peut
deviner la suite ?

Au bout du voyage
il y aura les visages
connus ou inconnus
Les yeux qui vont me boire
comme si j'étais le Messager
L'heure de lecture
où je m'absenterai
Les questions irritantes
auxquelles je me résoudrai à répondre
Le dîner décevant
Le vin approximatif
La compagne de table
qui ne saura sur quel pied danser
Les doutes d'après minuit
Et le lit
que je me résignerai à ouvrir
comme une tombe

that spread it
then withdrew from the canvas
Match his movement
And now
do you realize that it's darkness
that sees in you?

Vertigo sets in
Confusion thrusts its waves
Chaos has colors
an eye
Lovers gasp for breath
on a bed of clay and heat
An apple keeps falling
A name is given to water
then to fire
Creation hesitates
between the absolute weapon
and the most beautiful lamb in the world
Who can
guess what comes next?

At the end of the journey
there will be faces
known and unknown
Eyes that will drink my words
as if I were the Messenger
The hour of reading
when I will be absent
The exasperating questions
that I will agree to answer
The disappointing dinner
The middling wine
The woman sitting next to me
who will be flustered
The after midnight doubts
And the bed
I will climb into
like a tomb

Pourquoi un cheval
se cogne-t-il la tête
contre la porte ouverte de son box ?
Il veut qu'on ferme la porte
s'écria ta compagne
Personne dans le groupe n'émit d'objection
Cette version fut donc adoptée
Maintenant
tu te reposes la question :
Pourquoi un cheval
se cogne-t-il la tête
contre la porte ouverte de son box ?
Tu n'as pas plus de réponse
mais tu découvres avec effroi
que tu as
que tu as toujours eu
une tête de cheval

Oh que non
l'apaisement n'est pas venu
Il y a encore dans cette carcasse
un cortège de folies à naître
Il y a encore dans cette bouche
d'âcres profération
Il y a encore sur cette paume
des pistes interminables
pour la danse des malédictions
Il y a encore dans ce cœur
mille passions inassouvies
Il y a toi
amour
qui me recrées
quand je crois m'être éteint
Oh que non
l'apaisement n'est pas venu

J'attends mon arbre
Il y a bien là devant moi
ce palmier démuni

Why does a horse
knock its head
against the open door of its stall?
It wants the door closed
cried out your companion
No one in the group objected
Thus that version was adopted
Now
you ask yourself the question again:
Why does a horse knock its head
against the open door of its stall?
You don't have a better answer
but you discover with terror
that you have
that you have always had
a horse's head

Oh definitely not!
appeasement has not come
There is still in this carcass
a train of madnesses yet unborn
There are still in this mouth
scathing utterances
There are still on this palm
endless tracks
for the dance of curses
There is still in this heart
a thousand unfulfilled passions
There is you
love
who re-create me
when I think my fire has gone out
Oh definitely not!
appeasement has not come

I am waiting for my tree
There is just in front of me
that naked palm tree

et ce caoutchouc sans grâce
J'attends mon arbre
J'ai bien vu un fantôme de jardinier
planter là devant moi
une jeune pousse
dont je ne saurais nommer l'essence
J'attends mon arbre
J'ai bien rêvé cette nuit
d'un magnolia géant
avec des têtes coupées
en guise de fleurs
J'attends mon arbre
Et quand il sera là
le seul, l'unique
surgi d'un coup de foudre
je pourrai enfin
me remettre à écrire pour de bon

On m'a volé mon pays
Vous qui connaissez les lois
et savez vous battre
dites-moi
Où puis-je déposer une plainte
Qui pourra me rendre justice ?

Ce ne pourra pas être un pays
avec des drapeaux hissés
au-dessus des maisons
Une langue unique pour prier
Un nom que les tribuns prononcent
la bouche pleine de majuscules
en fermant les yeux de béatitude

Ce ne pourra pas être un pays
qu'il faille quitter ou retrouver
avec les mêmes déchirements
l'obscure litanie du deuil
et ce sanglot des racines
hélant d'improbables rivages

and that graceless rubber tree
I am waiting for my tree
I did see a ghost of a gardener
plant there in front of me
a young shoot
whose essence I could not name
I am waiting for my tree
I did dream last night
of a giant magnolia
with severed heads
for flowers
I am waiting for my tree
And when it is here
the one, the only
rising up from a bolt of lightning
I'll finally be able
to begin writing again
in earnest

They stole my country from me
You who know the laws
and who know how to fight
tell me
Where can I file a complaint
Who will do justice to me?

It cannot be a country
with flags hoisted
above the houses
A single language to pray in
A name the tribunes can utter
their mouths full of capital letters
while closing their eyes in bliss

It cannot be a country
you must leave or rediscover
with the same tearings
the dark litany of grief
and that sob from the roots
calling out from unlikely shores

Ce ne pourra pas être un pays
qu'on doive apprendre à l'école
à la caserne
en prison
avec la hantise
de se tromper de pays

Ce ne pourra pas être un pays
juste pour le ventre
ou la tombe
et rien d'autre
hormis le fardeau des peines
qu'on n'ose plus confier
même à l'ami

Ce ne pourra pas être un pays
qui ne sait plus rire
vivre à en être meurtri
peupler la nuit de ses excès
jusqu'à déchirer d'amour
les draps de l'aube

Ce ne pourra pas être un pays
parmi la cohorte des pays
cynique
avare
dur d'oreille
engraissant les voyous
leur offrant le glaive et la balance
alignant les suaires
et payant jusqu'aux pleureuses
pour les doux

Ce ne pourra pas être un pays
qui dans le cœur
chasse un autre pays
pour ériger des murailles
entre le désir et le désir

et vouer au blasphème
l'humble joie de l'errant

It cannot be a country
you must learn about at school
in the barracks
in prison
with the haunting fear
of being in
the wrong country

It cannot be a country
just for the belly
or the grave
and nothing else
except for the burden of sorrow
that you no longer dare to confide
even to your friend

It cannot be a country
that can no longer laugh
or live to bruising extremes
or people the night with its excesses
until tearing with love
the sheets of dawn

It cannot be a country
among the cohort of countries
cynical
miserly
hard of hearing
fattening up gangsters
offering them the sword and the scales
lining up the shrouds
and even hiring professional mourners
for the gentle ones

It cannot be a country
which in our heart
drives out another country
to erect walls
between desire and longing

and subject to blasphemy
the humble joy of the wanderer

Ce ne pourra pas être un pays
qui ferme sa porte à l'hôte
l'étranger
époux de l'étoile
émissaire de nos antiques amours
survivant de la marche
celle des origines
quand la vie nous visitait encore
et que nos pas s'aventuraient
de sillon en sillon
dans ce continent englouti
disparu
avant de nous livrer la clé du rêve
qu'il a fait glisser dans nos songes

Ah c'est un pays encore à naître
dans la soif et le dénuement
La brûlure qui rend l'âme à l'âme
et de la mer morte
des larmes
soulève la houle des mots

C'est un pays encore à naître
sur une terre coulant de source
éprise d'infini
drapée du bleu de l'enfance
aussi fraîche que la cascade
du premier soleil

C'est un pays encore à naître
dans la lenteur du lointain
et du proche
Dans la langueur de l'espérance
mille fois trahie
Dans la langue éperdue
et retrouvée

C'est un pays encore à naître
sur le chemin
qui ne fait que reprendre
et ne conduit à nul pays

It cannot be a country
that shuts its door to the guest
to the foreigner
spouse of the star
emissary of our ancient loves
survivor of the trek
the trek of origins
when life still visited us
and our steps ventured
from furrow to furrow
in the submerged continent
that disappeared
before handing over the key to the dream
it slipped into our reveries

Ah! it's a country yet to be born
in thirst and destitution
The burning that returns the soul to the soul
and from the dead sea
of tears
stirs up the storm of words

It's a country yet to be born
on an earth flowing naturally
enamored of the infinite
draped in the blue of childhood
as cool as the waterfall
of the first sun

It's a country yet to be born
in the slowness of the faraway
and the near
In the languor of hope
a thousand times betrayed
In the language bewildered
and rediscovered

It's a country yet to be born
on the path
which only begins again
and leads to no country

O pays qui m'écarte
et m'éloigne
Laisse-moi au moins te chercher

Casablanca-Rabat, 1995

O country that shuts me out
and distances me
Let me at least seek you

Casablanca-Rabat, 1995

POÈTE MIS À PART

Tu t'es retiré du monde
Peu à peu
le monde se retire de toi

Seul mon ami
et fier de l'être

Ton silence
parlera pour toi

Ici
l'eau t'entretient nuit et jour
Ta mémoire va se frotter à la sienne
Tes poissons vont s'y jeter
pour se reproduire
Tu vas lui dédier une vasque
des gondoles
et l'amphore de tes voluptés
Un jour
tu voudras que tes mots
deviennent son murmure

Le petit lac t'offre le luxe
d'un couple de cygnes
mais te donne pour tâche
de lui inventer une légende

A POET APART

You withdrew from the world
Little by little
the world withdraws from you

Alone my friend
and proud to be

Your silence
will speak for you

Here
the water speaks to you night and day
Your memory will rub against its memory
Your fish will jump in it
to multiply
You will dedicate a bowl to it
gondolas
and the amphora of your raptures
One day
you will want your words
to become its murmuring

The little lake offers you the luxury
of a couple of swans
but gives you the task
of inventing a legend for it

Pour une fois
tu as choisi ton désert
la taille de la blessure
l'ampleur de la perte
Désappartenir
En voilà une bataille !

Je vais dire une chose affreuse
Les pauvres sont souvent laids
Je l'ai dite la chose affreuse
J'ajoute que je n'aime pas les riches
les enfants de riches y compris
Je précise que je ne suis
ni riche ni pauvre
ni beau ni laid
J'ai simplement des envies
d'impertinence

Mon refuge donne sur un lac
dont on a vite fait le tour
Mais les pêcheurs y sont légion
Des adultes
des enfants
parfois une femme qui reste en retrait
pour admirer le savoir-faire des mâles
J'observe souvent cette activité cruelle
Que dis-je elle me fascine
On tue là sous mes yeux
et je ne lève pas le petit doigt
Je suis plutôt tenté
de quitter mon poste d'observation
me procurer une canne
et aller me joindre aux pêcheurs
ces prodiges de patience
ces petits tueurs sans prétention

For once
you have chosen your desert
the size of the wound
the breadth of the loss
To stop belonging
What a battle!

I am going to say a dreadful thing
The poor are often ugly
I have said it, the dreadful thing
Let me add that I do not like the wealthy
the offspring of the wealthy included
Let me make it clear that I am
neither rich nor poor
neither handsome nor ugly
I simply have cravings
for impertinence

My refuge looks out on a lake
which is not huge
But the fishermen are legion
Adults
children
sometimes a woman who stays in the background
to admire the skill of the males
I often observe this cruel activity
What can I say
it fascinates me
They are killing here before my eyes
and I don't lift a finger
I am tempted rather
to leave my observation post
find myself a fishing rod
and join the fishermen
these prodigies of patience
these little unpretentious killers

Le portrait du père
a pris sa place sur le mur
derrière moi
Je suis seul
dans ma chambre close
Ma femme est partie travailler
Pourtant
une main vient me caresser la nuque
doucement
telle une plume d'oiseau
Le goût de l'enfance
me monte à la bouche

La plante que j'ai mise sur le balcon
il y a une semaine
a grandi
et moi
je reste petit
Manquerais-je à ce point de terre
ou est-ce ma sève
qui est mauvaise ?

J'en viens à la légende des deux cygnes
Détrompez-vous
ce n'est pas une histoire d'amour
Ils sont frère et sœur
On les a amenés dans cette flaque
d'une cité de banlieue
pour que les humbles
se sentent moins humbles
et puissent dire fièrement à leurs enfants
drogués de télévision :
Regarde les jolis cygnes !
Et ces volatiles majestueux
et cruels paraît-il
font leur travail
comme d'honnêtes employés de la mairie
Maintenant va savoir

The portrait of the father
has taken its place on the wall
behind me
I am alone
in my closed room
My wife has left for work
Yet
a hand reaches out to caress
the nape of my neck
softly
like a bird's feather
The taste of childhood
rises in my mouth

The plant that I placed on the balcony
a week ago
has grown
and I
I remain small
Am I so deprived of soil
or is it my sap
that is bad?

I am getting to the legend of the two swans
You're wrong, though
it is not a love story
They are brother and sister
They were brought to this puddle
in the housing project
so that the humble ones
would feel less humble
and could proudly say to their children
drugged by televison:
Look at the pretty swans!
And these birds, majestic
and, they say, cruel
do their work
as honest municipal employees
Now how can you tell if

si nos héros n'entretiennent pas
par nécessité
une relation incestueuse

Pourquoi
fermes-tu ta porte quand tu écris ?
Tu ne voles pas
Tu ne tues pas
Tu ne mens pas
Tu ne fais rien de mal
sauf peut-être à toi
et encore
Alors pourquoi fermes-tu ta porte
As-tu peur
qu'un sosie maléfique entre
te jette par-dessus le balcon
et se mette à ta place
pour écrire
je ne sais quel roman à l'eau de rose
un traité révisionniste des passions
des poèmes cérébraux
bourrés de mots fatigués
tout cela signé de ton nom
Pourquoi fermes-tu ta porte
A cause du courant d'air dis-tu ?
Ça au moins c'est un mensonge

Dix fois le tour de la terre
et pas de havre en vue
Tourner tourner
tourner
Est-ce une vie ?

O pluies
si vous étiez
les larmes du ciel
je commencerais à croire

our heroes are not involved
by necessity
in an incestuous relationship

Why
do you shut your door when you write?
You don't steal
You don't kill
You don't lie
You do nothing bad
except maybe to yourself
and even so
Then why do you shut your door
Are you afraid
an evil double might enter
throw you over the balcony
and sit in your chair
to write
some sappy love story
a revisionist treatise of passions
cerebral poems
stuffed with tired words
and all signed in your name
Why do you close your door
Because of the draught you say?
That at least is a lie

Ten times around the earth
and no haven in sight
Turning round and round
and round
Is that a life?

Oh rains
if you were
the tears of the sky
I would begin to believe

Mère[1]
ma superbe
mon imprudente
Toi qui t'apprêtes à me mettre au monde
De grâce
ne me donne pas de nom
car les tueurs sont à l'affût

Mère
fais que ma peau
soit d'une couleur neutre
Les tueurs sont à l'affût

Mère
ne parle pas devant moi
Je risque d'apprendre ta langue
et les tueurs sont à l'affût

Mère
cache-toi quand tu pries
laisse-moi à l'écart de ta foi
Les tueurs sont à l'affût

Mère
libre à toi d'être pauvre
mais ne me jette pas dans la rue
Les tueurs sont à l'affût

Ah mère
si tu pouvais t'abstenir
attendre des jours meilleurs
pour me mettre au monde
Qui sait
Mon premier cri
ferait ma joie et la tienne
Je bondirais alors dans la lumière
comme une offrande de la vie à la vie

---

[1]A la mémoire de Brahim Bouarram, jeune Marocain qui fut poussé et noyé dans la Seine, à Paris, le 1er mai 1995, par une bande de skinheads qui venait de se détacher d'une manifestation du Front national.

Mother[1]
my proud
my foolhardy one
You who are about to bring me into this world
Please
do not give me a name
for the killers are on the watch

Mother
make my skin
of neutral color
The killers are on the watch

Mother
do not speak in my presence
I may risk learning your language
and the killers are on the watch

Mother
hide when you pray
keep me apart from your faith
The killers are on the watch

Mother
you are free to be poor
but do not throw me out on the street
The killers are on the watch

Ah mother
if you could abstain
wait for better days
to bring me into this world
Who knows
My first cry
might bring us both joy
I could then leap into the light
like an offering of life to life

---

[1]To the memory of Brahim Bouarram, a young Moroccan who was pushed into
the Seine and drowned in Paris, on May 1, 1995, by a gang of skinheads that had
detached itself from a demonstration of the National Front Party.

Accroche-toi
homme à la dérive
Il est des signes
à toi seul destinés
quand tu ne les attends pas
Ouvre ta main et tu verras
qu'une étoile s'est formée
entre la ligne de vie
et celle d'amour
Elle n'a que deux branches pour l'instant
mais c'est déjà une promesse
de ce que tu n'attends plus
Accroche-toi
homme à la dérive
Tes lignes
n'ont pas encore dit
leur dernier mot

Mon regard
n'engage personne
Je veille simplement
à ce qu'il m'engage
au moment du regard

Ton nom est étrange
quand les autres le prononcent
Il est encore plus étrange
quand c'est toi
qui le prononces

Ton visage
lui
n'arrête pas de te surprendre

Hang on
drifting man
There are signs
meant solely for you
when you do not expect them
Open your hand and you will see
a star has taken form
between the line of life
and the line of love
It has only two points for the moment
but that is already a promise
of what you no longer expect
Hang on
drifting man
Your lines
have not yet said
their last word

My gaze
binds no one
I am only careful
that it binds me
at the time of the gaze

Your name is strange
when others say it
It sounds even stranger
when you are the one
who say it.

Your face
for its part
never ceases to surprise you

Est-ce bien toi
que voilà
te disant « tu »
énigme en branle
dont le poème seul
se charge
tant bien que mal ?

D'où viens-tu mon brave
inconscient du risque
carcasse déjetée
livrée aux vents mauvais
d'une ère vouée toute à la ruse
Que viens-tu faire ici
sans armes
sans force
sans argent
Où veux-tu aller
de tes petits pas
de mutant mal dégrossi
Ne vois-tu pas
mon brave
que dans ta distraction
tu t'es trompé de galère ?

Les jeux ne sont jamais entièrement faits
réponds-tu
Les séismes n'avertissent pas
La force vieillit
moins vite que la beauté
mais elle vieillit
Tout ce qui paraît éternel
connaît une fin
plus ou moins glorieuse
plus ou moins ignominieuse
Aucune arme n'échappe
à la justice de la rouille
Les déshérités finissent par prendre
leur revanche

Is it really you
there
saying "you" to yourself
riddle in action
which only the poem
can handle
after a fashion?

Where do you come from my good man
unconscious of the peril
warped carcass
powerless amid the evil winds
of an era dedicated altogether to trickery
What have you come here for
without weapons
without strength
without money
Where are you heading for
toddling along
a still unpolished mutant
Don't you see
my good man
that in your absentmindedness
you boarded the wrong ship?

The die is never completely cast
you answer
Earthquakes do not send out warnings
Strength grows old
at a slower pace than beauty
but it grows old
Everything that seems eternal
has an end
more or less glorious
more or less ignominious
No weapon escapes
the justice of rust
The disinherited end up taking
their revenge

Le chemin tracé
n'est pas un chemin
Un vaisseau qui appareille
est toujours plus beau
qu'un vaisseau à quai

Qui a dit
que tu étais guéri du rêve ?
Aux abords du précipice
tu contemples encore le paysage
Dans ton cercueil
tu te vois vivant
Tu fermes les yeux pour retenir
ton premier rire de gisant
Tu profites d'un moment d'inattention
des mines éplorées qui t'entourent
pour subtiliser un crayon
et le glisser dans ta poche
Tu penses aux lettres bouleversantes
que tu enverras de l'inconnu
aux rares amis qui te restent
Qui a dit
que tu étais guéri de la vie ?

Pourtant
la salope
n'a pas été juste avec toi
Elle t'a eu
chaque fois que tu t'es donné à elle
Elle a toujours couru plus vite
que tes désirs les plus sincères
Que de pièges ne t'a-t-elle pas tendus
la grande farceuse
et quand tu te laissais prendre
tu te joignais au concert des moqueurs
au nom de la tolérance
Ça c'est de l'amour
ou je ne m'y connais pas

The road that is mapped
is not a path
A ship setting sail
is always lovelier
than a ship in dock

Who said
that you were cured of the dream?
At the edge of the abyss
you still gaze at the landscape
In your coffin
you see yourself alive
You close your eyes to hold back
your first laugh as a dead man
You seize a moment of inattention
in the weeping faces around you
to filch a pencil
and slip it into your pocket
You think of the deeply moving
letters you will send from the unknown
to your few remaining friends
Who said
that you were cured of life?

Yet
the bitch
has not been fair with you
She conned you
every time you gave yourself to her
She always ran faster
than your most sincere desires
How many traps hasn't she set for you
the great trickster
and whenever you fell into one
you would join the chorus of scoffers
in the name of tolerance
Now if that isn't true love
I don't know what is

Je voudrais garder une image
ne serait-ce qu'une seule
de cette enfance
de ce pays
de cette vie chaotique
Facile à dire
Que de nuits me faudrait-il consumer
Que de jours devrais-je supporter
cette montagne sur la langue
Que de pages devrais-je arracher
aux autres pages
pour entrevoir des écritures à l'envers
des couleurs cachées sous une aile
les sabots d'une sirène sans visage
le double fond de la valise
où je verrais
où je verrais quoi ?

Ce ne sont que prémices
et débris
d'une image
qui n'a pas encore lieu d'être
tant la blessure est vive
Et pour en saisir le bout du fil
il faudrait
de mes yeux
vider entièrement ce lac
couvrir le ciel
d'un rideau noir
peindre les arbres en blanc
interdire la zone aux enfants
allumer des cierges autour de mes livres
invoquer la foudre
et le glaive de l'Imam païen
Bref
revivre l'horreur
la traîtrise
l'agonie d'un peuple livré aux voyous

I would like to keep a picture
if only just this one
of this childhood
of this country
of this chaotic life
Easy to say
So many nights I would have to consume
So many days I would have to endure
this mountain on my tongue
So many pages I would have to tear
from the other pages
to glimpse writings upside down
colors hidden beneath a wing
the clogs of a faceless mermaid
the double bottom of the suitcase
where I would see
where I would see what?

These are only beginnings
and debris
of an image
that has not yet emerged
so sharp is the wound
And to grasp its thread
I would have to
empty this lake entirely
with my eyes
cover the sky
with a dark curtain
paint the trees white
make the area off limits to children
light candles around my books
invoke the lightning
and the pagan Imam's sword
In short
relive the horror
the betrayal
the agony of a people surrendered to gangsters

Il faudrait être si fort
et je suis faible
Je n'ai que l'énergie
de l'escarbille qui éclate
entre deux silences
le vouloir du convalescent
qui caresse le fruit
déposé depuis longtemps à son chevet
le désir convulsif
du monstre endormi par désenchantement
Il faudrait être si fort
quand j'ai besoin
de me familiariser avec ma faiblesse

L'histoire des deux cygnes
n'est pas terminée
Et d'abord qui me dit que ce sont les mêmes
que je retrouve chaque matin
quand j'ouvre ma fenêtre
Qui sait si la déesse de l'amour
ne les a pas remplacés la nuit dernière
par un couple célèbre
ou qui va l'être ?
A moins qu'ils ne soient deux robots parfaits
que le dieu de l'électronique
a placés là
pour me convertir à l'illusion
et me faire célébrer
sa gloire

Le voisin
a repris son bricolage
Que veut-il m'enfoncer dans le crâne
avec son marteau ?
Si ça continue
j'irai sonner à sa porte
pour lui dire :
Je vous en prie monsieur

I should be so strong
and I am weak
I only have the energy
of a cinder bursting
between two silences
the will of a convalescent
stroking the fruit
left long ago at his bedside
the convulsive desire
of a monster put to sleep by disillusion
I should be so strong
when I need
to get to know my weakness

The story of the two swans
is not finished
And to begin with
who says they are the same ones
I see every morning
when I open my window
Who knows if the goddess of love
has not replaced them the night before
with a pair that is famous
or soon to be?
Unless they are two perfect robots
that the god of electronics
has placed there
to convert me to the illusion
and make me sing
his praise

The neighbor
is working on his place again
What does he want to drive into my skull
with his hammer?
If this goes on
I will go and ring his doorbell
and tell him:
Please sir

n'insistez pas
J'ai mes propres idées

Eh
Et si mon voisin était une femme
une beauté de surcroît
qui viendrait m'ouvrir en petite tenue
que lui dirais-je ?

Un des cygnes a disparu
Ma femme en est sûre
L'a-t-on volé
Est-il mort
Que va devenir son compagnon ?
D'après la légende
il ne tardera pas à mourir lui aussi
La séparation tue chez les cygnes
Je ne savais donc pas que j'observais
une espèce supérieure
que je jetais du pain rassis
à mes maîtres en amour

Le ciel m'a vidé
J'ai vidé le lac
Les mots ont donné
et j'ai donné

L'appétit revient
ma chair est presque délicieuse

Ce n'est qu'un autre livre
qui se referme sur moi
comme une cellule de verre

Boissy-Saint-Léger, 1995

don't push it
I have my own ideas

Well
And if my neighbor were a woman
and a beautiful one to boot
who came to the door in skimpy attire
what would I say to her?

One of the swans has disappeared
My wife is sure of that
Has it been stolen
Is it dead
What will happen to its companion?
According to the legend
before long it too will die
In the world of swans, separation kills
I did not know then that I was observing
a superior species
that I was throwing stale bread
to my masters in love

The sky has emptied me
I have emptied the lake
The words have given
and I have given

Appetite returns
my flesh is almost delicious

It is only another book
closing over me
like a glass cell

Boissy-Saint-Léger, 1995

LA TERRE S'OUVRE ET T'ACCUEILLE

A la mémoire de Tahar Djaout,*
le jour de son enterrement

La terre s'ouvre
et t'accueille
Pourquoi ces cris, ces larmes
ces prières
Qu'ont-ils perdu
Que cherchent-ils
ceux-là qui troublent
ta paix retrouvée ?

La terre s'ouvre
et t'accueille
Maintenant
vous allez vous parler sans témoins
Oh vous en avez des choses à vous raconter
et vous aurez l'éternité pour le faire
Les mots d'hier ternis par le tumulte
vont peu à peu se graver dans le silence

La terre s'ouvre
et t'accueille
Elle seule t'a désiré
sans que tu lui fasses des avances
Elle t'a attendu sans ruse de Pénélope
Sa patience ne fut que bonté
et c'est la bonté qui te ramène à elle

La terre s'ouvre
et t'accueille
Elle ne te demandera pas de comptes
sur tes amours éphémères
filles de l'errance
étoiles de chair conçues dans les yeux
fruits accordés du vaste verger de la vie
souveraines passions qui font soleil

---

*Ecrivain algérien assassiné en 1993 à Alger par des fanatiques

THE EARTH OPENS AND WELCOMES YOU

*To the memory of Tahar Djaout**
on the day of his funeral

The earth opens
and welcomes you
Why these cries, these tears
these prayers
What have they lost
What are they looking for
those who trouble
your refound peace?

The earth opens
and welcomes you
Now
you will converse without witnesses
O you have things to tell each other
and you'll have eternity to do so
Yesterday's words tarnished by the tumult
will one by one engrave themselves on silence

The earth opens
and welcomes you
She alone has desired you
without you making any advances
She has waited for you without Penelopian ruses
Her patience was but goodness
and it is goodness brings you back to her

The earth opens
and welcomes you
She won't ask you to account
for your ephemeral loves
daughters of errancy
flesh stars conceived in the eyes
accorded fruits from the vast orchard of life
sovereign passions that make sun

---

*Algerian journalist and author murdered by fanatics in Algiers in 1993

au creux de la paume
au bout de la langue éperdue

La terre s'ouvre et t'accueille
Tu es nu
Elle est encore plus nue que toi
Et vous êtes beaux
dans cette étreinte muette
où les mains savent se retenir
pour écarter la violence
où le papillon de l'âme
se détourne de ce semblant de lumière
pour aller en quête de sa source

La terre s'ouvre
et t'accueille
Ta bien-aimée retrouvera un jour
ton sourire légendaire
et le deuil prendra fin
Tes enfants grandiront
et liront sans gêne tes poèmes
Ton pays guérira comme par miracle
lorsque les hommes épuisés par l'illusion
iront s'abreuver à la fontaine de ta bonté

O mon ami
dors bien
tu en as besoin
car tu as travaillé dur
en honnête homme
Avant de partir
tu as laissé ton bureau propre
bien rangé
Tu as éteint les lumières
dit un mot gentil au gardien
Et puis en sortant
tu as regardé le ciel
son bleu presque douloureux
Tu as lissé élégamment ta moustache
en te disant :
seuls les lâches
considèrent que la mort est une fin

in the palm's hollow
at the tip of the tipsy tongue

The earth opens
and welcomes you
You are naked
She is even more naked than you
And you are both beautiful
in that silent embrace
where the hands know how to hold back
to avoid violence
where the soul's butterfly
turns away from this semblance of light
to go in search of its source

The earth opens
and welcomes you
Your loved one will find again some day
your legendary smile
and the mourning will be over
Your children will grow up
and will read your poems without shame
Your country will heal as if by miracle
when the men exhausted by illusion
will go drink from the fountain of your goodness

O my friend
sleep well
you need it
for you have worked hard
as an honest man
Before leaving
you left your desk clean
well ordered
You turned off the lights
said a nice word to the guardian
And then as you stepped out
you looked at the sky
its near-painful blue
You elegantly smoothed your mustache
telling yourself:
only cowards
consider death to be an end

Dors bien mon ami
Dors du sommeil du juste
Repose-toi, même de tes rêves
Laisse-nous porter un peu le fardeau

Créteil, le 4 juin 1993

Sleep well my friend
Sleep the sleep of the just
Get some rest, even from your dreams
Let us for awhile carry the burden

Créteil, June 4, 1993

ABOUT THE TRANSLATORS

Anne George, a native of France, holds a Ph.D. in comparative literature from the University of Washington. Presently an assistant professor at Seattle University, she has been actively engaged in interviewing and videotaping literary artists from Quebec and the Maghreb; the latter includes an hour-long interview with Abdellatif Laâbi.

Edris Makward is an Emeritis Professor of French and African Literatures from the University of Wisconsin at Madison. He is currently Dean of the Faculty of Humanities and Social Sciences and Deputy Vice-Chancellor at the newly established University of The Gambia, his place of birth in West Africa.

Victor Reinking teaches French and African literature at Seattle University, where he is also chair of the Department of Modern Languages. He is currently working on a book, *The Poetics of Prison in Four African Writers: Nawal El Saadawi, Wole Soyinka, Abdellatif Laâbi, and Ngugi wa Thiong'o.*

Pierre Joris has published many books of poetry, among them *Poasis: Selected Poems 1986–1999*. His translations include books by Paul Celan, Maurice Blanchot, Edmond Jabès, Abdelwaab Meddeb, Habib Tengor, and Kurt Schwitters. With Jerome Rothenberg he edited *The Poems of the Millennium* anthologies. *A nomad poetics,* a collection of essays, will be published by Wesleyan in 2003.